Patterns for Bapti

Patterns for Baptism

Church House Publishing

Published by   Church House Publishing
               Church House
               Great Smith Street
               London SW1P 3AZ

Copyright ©   The Archbishops' Council 2006, 2015, 2022

               First published 2022

               Some of the material in this book is extracted from *Common Worship: Christian Initiation* (2006) and *Common Worship: Christian Initiation. Additional Baptism Texts in Accessible Language* (2015).

               ISBN 978 0 7151 2349 2

Printed and bound in Great Britain by Bell and Bain Ltd, Glasgow

Typeset by Hugh Hillyard-Parker, Edinburgh

Common Worship design by Derek Birdsall RDI and John Morgan

PATTERNS FOR BAPTISM

Contents

The Liturgy of the Eucharist

The Sending Out

Other texts

Sample Services Section

Sample Services

Guidance Notes for Particular Circumstances

Scenarios

Introduction

Introduction to this Volume

Common Worship initiation material was first published in 1998, as *Common Worship: Initiation Services*. General Synod subsequently made amendments to some of the rubrics, which had the effect of making more parts of the service optional and giving more choices. The basic form of baptism service published in the *Common Worship* main volume in 2000 reflected these changes.

In 2006 a new volume, *Common Worship: Christian Initiation*, was published, which provided more material (adding material to the volume, such as rites for the reconciliation of a penitent, and 'Rites on the Way'), as well as incorporating the earlier amendments into the full range of services.

In 2015, General Synod approved further optional texts, *Additional Baptism Texts in Accessible Language*. These (like the other *Common Worship* texts) were made available on the Church of England website, and were also published in booklet form.

The result of all of this is that the *Common Worship* initiation services (and especially Holy Baptism) provide a flexible set of resources, which can be adapted to fit a range of different pastoral contexts. However, one of the implications of that flexibility is that the material is also very complex, and it is not always easy for clergy and others to find the full range of material and to be sure about what the options now are. This is because while some options are clear in the text or indicated by rubrics, others only become apparent from the formidable Notes at the end of the services.

Though the range of options applies across all the initiation services, the most pressing context in which this makes an impact is in baptism services in local churches, fresh expressions of church and chaplaincies. This volume is therefore focused on the options for baptism services, rather than the full range of initiation services. It is designed to be used alongside the new *Common Worship: Baptism and Confirmation* volume, which includes the other initiation material (including confirmation, affirmation of baptismal faith and reception into the Church of England).

Patterns for Baptism brings together all of the authorized *Common Worship* baptismal material in one volume, making all of the options clear for each part of the service and including some guidance notes and commentary. Some of this guidance is newly written, but some is adapted from the rubrics or notes to the services, and some from commentary previously produced by the Liturgical Commission. The full Notes to the *Common Worship* texts (where many of the options and flexibility lie) are also reproduced in full after each structure page and at the end of all the resources. This is, then, a planning document, rather than a document from which to lead worship.

In the Resource Section, each prayer or other item is given a code (e.g. G3). This is designed to make it easier to be clear exactly which option is being referred to when planning a service. It is also designed to make it easier to find the material when searching the Church of England website, where all the material is also available. The aim is to enable local worship leaders to bring material together easily and to produce forms of service which reflect the appropriate use of the authorized material in their own locality.

Introduction to Baptism in *Common Worship*

The rediscovery of baptism and its importance

Over the last hundred years or so, there has been a significant rediscovery of the meaning and significance of baptism by Christians around the world and in different Churches. Before this, baptism was often treated as a sort of birth rite within a Christian society. Where there was controversy it often reflected other anxieties – such as the nature of salvation, the importance of personal faith, or a desire to clarify the boundaries of the Church in a more sceptical culture – rather than an appreciation of the theological importance of baptism itself. Various factors have contributed to a revival of baptismal theology: worldwide mission, patristic and biblical study, the changing social context of the Church, to name but some.

There was a tendency to see baptism as an isolated moment in the individual Christian life and as the gateway (via confirmation) to the eucharist, itself the one proper sacramental focus of the Christian life. Increasingly baptism is seen as a sacrament of significance in its own right that points Christians to their true identity, character and calling within the body of Christ. The apostle Paul repeatedly refers his hearers back to baptism, not simply as a reminder of their conversion but as a way of bringing home to them what it is to be in Christ.

A theological framework

Inspired by the widespread rediscovery of baptism, the Liturgical Commission worked with the following biblical framework when preparing the services in *Common Worship*, believing that baptism involves:

- *separation* from all that alienates us from God, and
- *reception* into a universal community centred on God,
- whose *mission* is to serve God's Spirit in redeeming the world, and
- within which we can *grow* into the fullness of the pattern of Christ.

This baptismal framework is communicated in Scripture through a rich tapestry of imagery. Some images cover part of the process; others provide an interpretative picture for the whole. All have a claim to be reflected within any liturgy of baptism; some need to be highlighted either in the preparation for baptism or in reflection after the celebration of baptism.

The following table indicates the richness and breadth of that tapestry of scriptural imagery:

Theme	Imagery	Bible reference
liberation	liberation	Exodus 1 Corinthians 10.1-4
	rescue from the power of darkness and sin	Colossians 1.12-14 Revelation 1.5
new creation	new creation	Galatians 6.15 2 Corinthians 5.17
	liberation from Babylon as a new exodus and new creation, defeating the dragon of chaos	Isaiah 51.9-11 Genesis 1.2
new birth	'from above', of water and the Spirit	John 3.3ff 1 Peter 1.3,23 James 1.18
reconciliation	removal of enmity	Romans 5.6-11 2 Corinthians 5.18 – 6.2
illumination	illumination	2 Corinthians 4.4-6 Genesis 1.3
	opening of eyes, ears, hearts and minds	Ephesians 1.18 Hebrews 6.4 John 9
recognition	receiving the name of Christ	James 2.7 Isaiah 43.1
cleansing	washing	Ephesians 5.26 Hebrews 10.22 Titus 3.5
	removal of defilement	Romans 3.25 1 John 2.2; 4.10

Theme	Imagery	Bible reference
stripping	putting off the old human	Colossians 3.9
	the Christian analogue to circumcision	Colossians 2.11
clothing	putting on Christ	Galatians 3.27
	the new human	Colossians 3.10
dying	drowning, burial	Romans 6.3ff Colossians 2.12
	participation in Christ's 'exodus'	Luke 9.31
	the ordeal foreshadowed in his own baptism	Luke 12.50 Mark 10.38
resurrection	into newness of life	Romans 6.4ff Colossians 2.12; 3.1ff
building	as living stones into a new temple/community	1 Corinthians 3.9ff Ephesians 2.19-21 1 Peter 2.4ff

Accessible language and rich imagery

The full and rich biblical imagery surrounding baptism and the comparative ignorance of this richness in many sections of modern society pose a major problem in the drafting of services of Christian initiation. A common way of resolving this difficulty has been to select one biblical image, commonly that of death and resurrection, and play down other major scriptural emphases. In particular, this has meant the marginalization of many important themes associated with the baptism of Christ that are taken up in the New Testament in the feast of Pentecost: the kingdom of God, identification with the passion of Christ, the coming of the Holy Spirit, incorporation into the life of the Trinity and the mission of God in the world.

In framing the *Common Worship* services the intention was to hold a balance between, on the one hand, a richer use of biblical types and allusions in presidential texts and, on the other, the sort of language and phrasing that could reasonably be put into the mouths of parents, godparents, sponsors and congregation. The provision of additional texts, deliberately written in more accessible language, has been a further response to the need to be accessible while remaining true to the range of images in Scripture.

Local choices about which of the options to use will need to take account of these issues, and how they may best be balanced in particular contexts or pastoral situations.

Seasonal provision

One of the ways of expanding the range of imagery, especially in presidential texts, has been to provide a range of seasonally focused forms of words. The ancient Church of the West has traditionally associated baptism with Easter. However, other traditions in the Church have associated baptism with other times in the Church year, particularly the Epiphany and the Baptism of Christ, and All Saints' tide. The *Common Worship* services therefore provide resources for baptisms at any time ('General') as well as forms of words which connect with the baptismal themes which might be particularly appropriate in the seasons of Eastertide, Epiphany and All Saints' tide.

One baptism service for adults and infants

Though there are variations that take account of different candidates and their needs (for instance, words for parents and godparents to say at the baptism of an infant), the overall shape and journey through the service is the same for all candidates. This makes clear that there is only one baptism which brings people into relationship with Christ and his Church: 'one Lord, one faith, one baptism' (Ephesians 4.5).

This emphasis on one baptism has been a theme of the modern rediscovery of baptism. For both infants and adults the service has the same inner logic, a movement from welcome and renunciation through to an identification with the people of God in their dependence on God, their profession of the saving name, and the common activities of prayer, eucharist and mission. The different life circumstances of the newly baptized find expression in the different form that the Commission takes in each case.

The importance of the human story in baptism

In Acts 9.1-31 Paul's conversion is not complete with the dramatic religious experience described in verses 3-9. It reaches its conclusion with verse 19, after the church in Damascus has played its part in the welcome and incorporation of the new believer.

The passage also indicates the importance of stories and storytelling in Christian experience and therefore in Christian initiation. The story of Paul's conversion is told three times in Acts. Christian initiation cannot be reduced to doctrinal and moral instruction or liturgical rites; it must include the narrative of rounded human experience. Each individual's story needs to be heard and to find its place within the unfolding story of faith in the Church and in the Scriptures. There must, therefore, be appropriate space in the processes surrounding baptism for the telling and retelling of human stories.

The giving of testimony in baptism services is one way of encouraging this. For those able to speak for themselves this will mean their own story; where candidates are not able to speak for themselves, parents, godparents or sponsors can speak of why they have sought baptism for the candidate. Confirmation then becomes a later opportunity for the candidate to affirm that the journey of Christian faith has become their own.

Godparents and sponsors

The Canons of the Church of England (Canon B 23) recognize both sponsors, who support candidates for baptism, and godparents, who take on their role at the baptism of children. The baptism service recognizes both a social and a spiritual role for godparents in the lives of their godchildren. The minister can dispense godparents from the normal requirement that a godparent should be confirmed. It is possible for a child to have additional sponsors as well as godparents who also agree to support them in their continuing journey to a mature faith.

Parental faith and proxy speaking

A key question for any Church that baptizes infants as well as adult believers is how parental faith relates to the baptism of children.

The Book of Common Prayer is notable for the absence of any explicit demand for parental faith, whereas *The Alternative Service Book 1980* asked parents and godparents to acknowledge that they spoke 'for themselves and for these children' in making the baptismal renunciations and profession of faith. There are two issues of substance lying behind these contrasting approaches.

The first is the legitimacy of bracketing together the parents' and infant's baptismal profession. This risks disguising the real commitment to Christ being made on behalf of the child in the act of baptism, a matter which stands out clearly in *The Book of Common Prayer* and the tradition which precedes it, and which is focused in the ancient practice of proxy vows. There is also an objection to requiring that parents should make a personal baptismal commitment at the moment when the child, and not themselves, is the focus of the service.

The second is the question of whether a requirement of parental faith is based on primarily pastoral or primarily theological grounds. Some, for instance, have appeared to argue on theological grounds that only the children of believers are within God's covenant of grace. However, the strong New Testament insistence that membership of the people of God is not a matter of blood or racial descent, and the fact that 'household' baptism appears to have included slaves and clients as well as blood relatives, suggests that any such requirement has to be defended on pastoral grounds. It must rest on the pastoral judgement that, in this social context, the child's most likely chance of the meaningful Christian nurture implied by its baptism is the full involvement of a believing parent. One of the challenges of this pastoral defence is that it does not take seriously the starting point of many parents who bring their child to the Church for baptism, and therefore risks asking too much too soon and forcing people to make statements in the service for which they are not yet ready.

These issues were discussed at length during the synodical process that produced the *Common Worship* baptism service. The final form of the service deals with questions to parents and godparents separately from the candidate's baptismal renunciation, and returns to the classic form of proxy vows, spoken in the name of an infant candidate, at the Decision. Such proxy vows reflect the fact that in other areas of life too, parents often make decisions or speak on behalf of their children, committing them to particular life choices until they are old enough to make their own decision – either to make that commitment their own, or to opt out of it. This can happen, for instance, in a range of ways, from commitments to a particular sport or team, through to significant ethical choices, such as vegetarianism or a commitment to Fairtrade goods. Confirmation clearly has an important role to play, in the case of baptism, in allowing an infant candidate to make the commitment their own, in due course.

The earlier questions at the Presentation of the Candidates, however, are addressed directly to parents and godparents. These questions presuppose a committed Christian faith while recognizing that in practice the extent of such faith is often limited or unarticulated, and that the active tasks of bringing a child to church will require the support of parents, but may lie in hands of churchgoing godparents, grandparents, neighbours, or family friends.

The Commission (either in one of the forms provided in the service, or articulated more informally in the sermon) has an important further role in spelling out the implications of baptism for those supporting infant candidates in the journey of faith.

It is presupposed that good pastoral practice will include an appropriate explanation of this to the parents, godparents and sponsors in advance of the service itself, along with the offer of whatever support the local church can provide.

The use of oil in baptism

The *Common Worship* services of baptism allow for the use of oil and indicate two customary places where this can occur: at the Signing with the Cross after the Decision, and immediately following the baptism itself, to accompany the prayer for grace and renewal by the Holy Spirit. In the first position, the oil used is pure olive oil; in the second it can be oil scented with fragrant spices (sometimes known as 'chrism'). In neither place is the use of oil compulsory.

Though the 'blessing of oils' has become a common feature in the Maundy Thursday services of many dioceses, it is not essential for the oils used in baptism to have been blessed by the bishop in this way.

The practice of using oil in association with the rite of baptism has its origin in the natural use of olive oil in Mediterranean culture and draws on rich scriptural imagery. The application of oil to the body had a number of distinct uses. Oil was used for healing and to prepare and soften an athlete's body for the contest. It was associated with washing and was used to cleanse and protect the body. It also functioned as a sign of blessing, empowerment and joy. The increasing use of oils for cosmetic or healing purposes in modern culture marks an interesting point of contact with older practice. These practices in biblical cultures provide the background for the use of oil in the anointing of prophets, priests and kings. Theologically one of its most important uses, the anointing of a king, gives us the title Christ (Messiah), the anointed one. Oil made fragrant with spices (chrism) has therefore been used in a variety of Christian traditions as a sign of participation in the community of the anointed one and in the royal priesthood of the Church.

In the historic Western tradition pure olive oil has been used before baptism as part of the preparation of the Christian athlete for the struggle of faith. Chrism has been used in rites that follow baptism as a sign of the blessings brought by the Holy Spirit. However, it is important to recognize that within the wider Christian tradition, there has been a more varied range of understandings and usage. There is, for instance, an ancient Eastern tradition which only used oil before baptism but understood this use as a messianic anointing.

The Western tradition has tended to associate the use of chrism with confirmation, but the view has been taken in these services that it is consistent with the Western tradition not to *limit* the use of chrism in this way, not least because of the association of the Holy Spirit with baptism itself. The use of chrism is therefore also allowed after baptism (as well as at services of affirmation of baptismal faith and at reception into the communion of the Church of England). This does not imply either that these are confirmation in the sense in which the law and formularies of the Church of England use this term, or that the use of the oil of chrism is essential to confirmation. However, for the sake of symbolic coherence, if a service includes baptism along with one or more of confirmation, affirmation or reception, the oil of chrism should only be applied once to any individual candidate in that service.

The baptism of adults and admission to communion

When adults are baptized the Canons of the Church of England (Canon B 15A) allow them to be admitted to communion when they are 'confirmed or ready and desirous to be confirmed'. This allows two practices.

- In the first the adult is baptized and confirmed by the bishop in the one service and so admitted to communion (at this or a subsequent service).

- In the second the adult is baptized in the parish (the Bishop having been notified at least a week before – Canon B 24.2) and subsequently brought to the bishop for confirmation. He or she may be admitted to communion after the baptism, or this can be delayed until after the confirmation if desired.

STRUCTURE SECTION

Structure Section

Introduction to the Structure Section

One of the key emphases in the *Common Worship* services is the importance of structure and shape. Each service across the range of *Common Worship* material begins with an outline of the structure before presenting the full service.

This volume takes the same approach, beginning by presenting four different structures for a baptism service. These structure pages have been kept as simple as possible to make the shape of the service clear. The hope is that by seeing the nature of the journey through the service, worship leaders will be equipped to help congregations as they navigate their way through what can appear to be a complicated act of worship.

The structures therefore act like a series of skeletons or outlines. Having established the shape of the service, planners then need to turn to the Resource Section in order to find the material to 'clothe' the outline and form a full service appropriate for the particular context.

That service will need other material too, of course – music, song, 'mood', movement, and symbol. The Resource Section in this volume focuses on the liturgical texts authorized for use in the Church of England, but the full service will benefit from attention being paid to the other aspects too. Some of those further aspects are explored in the Sample Services Section, especially in the scenarios, which consider a variety of possible contexts and needs, and how a local church can think creatively about more than simply the texts of the service.

Many of the elements of a baptism service have alternative positions. In the structure pages that follow, these elements have been indicated with an asterisk (*). The alternative positions have not been indicated in the structure pages themselves because this would make them over-complicated. Instead, the default position for each element is indicated, and the asterisk serves to remind service planners to check the Resource Section where there is clear information about alternative positions.

Baptism – Structure 1
(within a service of Holy Communion)

This gives the basic structure of the service, with items in the Common Worship default positions.

Items marked with an asterisk (*) have alternative positions – see the commentary in the relevant resource sections below for details.

Structure 1

¶ Preparation

The Greeting

[Thanksgiving Prayer for a Child – *optional*]

Introduction to Baptism

The Collect

¶ The Liturgy of the Word

[Readings and Psalm – *optional*]

Gospel Reading

Sermon

¶ The Liturgy of Baptism

Presentation of the Candidates *

The Decision

Signing with the Cross *

Prayer over the Water

Profession of Faith

Baptism

Commission *

Prayers of Intercession *

The Welcome and Peace

¶ The Liturgy of the Eucharist

Preparation of the Table
Taking of the Bread and Wine
The Eucharistic Prayer
The Lord's Prayer
Breaking of the Bread
Giving of Communion
Prayer after Communion

¶ The Sending Out

The Blessing
Giving of a Lighted Candle *
The Dismissal

Notes

The notes are reproduced here in the form authorized by General Synod in the original Common Worship *services. Where this is now incomplete because of the provision in the Additional Baptism Texts in Accessible Language, this has been indicated by a supplementary comment, presented in italic within square brackets, [...].*

The service for Holy Baptism provides for baptism in the context of the celebration of Holy Communion. The following notes aim to highlight the implication of this for baptism at a parish's regular Sunday celebration of Holy Communion.

1 The opening of the service should include an appropriate introduction and may include a prayer of thanksgiving for the child.

2 The Prayers of Penitence and the Nicene Creed are omitted.

3 The Presentation of the Candidates for Baptism takes place after the sermon. Alternatively it may form part of the opening section of the service; before the Gloria or Kyries (where these are used). If the presentation is used in this earlier position, it must precede the Collect.

4 Baptism takes place after the sermon.

5 An interrogatory version of the Apostles' Creed is provided in the text, to be said by the whole congregation. The Apostles' Creed is the normal baptismal creed in the Western tradition. A shorter Profession of Faith can be found at item J2, page 93.

6 The first form of the Commission is to be used at the baptism of children. The second form is to be used at the baptism of those able to answer for themselves. *[The Additional Baptismal Texts provide further options, which are included in this volume. The two forms mentioned in this note are items L1 and L3 in this volume.]*

7 A brief form of the Prayers of Intercession is provided. Longer and seasonal forms are to be found on pages 114–123. The Prayers may be placed before or after the Welcome. If the Prayers precede the Welcome and Peace, the Liturgy of the Eucharist then continues in the usual way with the Preparation of the Table and the Taking of the Bread and Wine.

8 A lighted candle is presented to the newly baptized as part of the conclusion of the service. It may be appropriate to invite the parents and godparents to the front at this point. The candle is lit from the Paschal candle (or other large candle) previously lit at the Decision.

The following table indicates how the service for Holy Baptism is to be used with the services indicated.

Order of Baptism	Order One	Order Two / BCP
[Thanksgiving] Introduction	After the Greeting [omit Prayers of Penitence]	After the Sermon
	Omit Nicene Creed	Omit Nicene Creed
Presentation	After the Greeting or Sermon	After the Introduction
Baptism	After the Sermon	After the Presentation
Prayers of Intercession	At the Intercessions [omit Prayers of Penitence]	Use Prayers of Intercession from Holy Baptism in place of Prayer for Church Militant
Welcome and Peace	At the Peace	Use the Welcome after the Commission
Prayer after Communion	After the Giving of Bread and Wine	Do not use
Giving of a Lighted Candle	Between the Blessing and Dismissal	After the Blessing

Baptism – Structure 2 (without Holy Communion)

This gives the basic structure of the service, with items in the Common Worship default positions. Though this structure can be used for a baptism service that forms a non-eucharistic main Sunday service, Structure 3 would be another alternative for that situation.

Structure 2 might naturally form the basis of a baptism service which (for pastoral reasons) cannot take place within a main Sunday service.

Items marked with an asterisk (*) have alternative positions – see the commentary in the relevant Resource sections below for details.

¶ Preparation

The Greeting

[Thanksgiving Prayer for a Child – *optional*]

Introduction to Baptism

The Collect

¶ The Liturgy of the Word

[Readings and Psalm – *optional*]

Gospel Reading

Sermon

¶ The Liturgy of Baptism

Presentation of the Candidates *

The Decision

Signing with the Cross *

Prayer over the Water

Profession of Faith

Baptism

Commission *

The Welcome and Peace

Prayers of Intercession *

The Lord's Prayer

¶ **The Sending Out**

The Blessing
Giving of a Lighted Candle *
The Dismissal

Baptism – Structure 3 (at A Service of the Word)

The headings in the service structure are primarily those from A Service of the Word, incorporating appropriate sections from the service of Holy Baptism.

This is the structure that would give the maximum flexibility for baptism as part of a non-eucharistic main Sunday service.

Items from the baptismal liturgy marked with an asterisk (*) have particular alternative positions, but as with any act of worship based on A Service of the Word, the structure given below is not the only one possible.

¶ Preparation

The Greeting

Venite, Gloria, a hymn, song or set of responses may be used.

The Collect *

¶ The Liturgy of the Word

Readings (or a reading) from Holy Scripture

A Psalm, or, if occasion demands, a scriptural song

Sermon

¶ The Liturgy of Baptism

[Thanksgiving Prayer for a Child – *optional*]

Introduction to Baptism *

Presentation of the Candidates *

The Decision

Signing with the Cross *

Prayer over the Water

Profession of Faith

Baptism

Commission *

The Welcome and Peace

¶ Prayers

These include

Intercessions and Thanksgivings *
The Lord's Prayer

¶ Conclusion

The service concludes with a blessing, dismissal or other liturgical ending.

The Blessing
Giving of a Lighted Candle *
The Dismissal

Notes

Any minister may preside over A Service of the Word, the Prayers and the Commission. The minister of baptism, who is the parish priest or other minister authorized to administer Holy Baptism, must preside over the Liturgy of Baptism.

Where alternative forms are provided in the service for Holy Baptism, they may be used with A Service of the Word.

1 The Prayers of Penitence are not used.

2 The Creed or Affirmation of Faith is replaced by the Profession of Faith.

3 The following may be used as part of the Preparation or after the Liturgy of the Word:

> Thanksgiving Prayer for a Child
> The Introduction
> Presentation of the Candidates

4 After the Liturgy of the Word, the Liturgy of Baptism follows, omitting the Presentation of the Candidates, if used earlier, and the Prayers of Intercession, if they are to be used later.

5 The Prayers of Intercession may be used before or after the Welcome or later in the service.

6 The Giving of a Lighted Candle takes place at the conclusion of the service. Alternatively it may take place after the administration of baptism.

The Notes to the service for Holy Baptism (pages 162–166) apply to the Thanksgiving Prayer for a Child, the Liturgy of Baptism and the Giving of a Lighted Candle.

Baptism – Structure 4
(at Morning or Evening Prayer)

This gives the basic structure when baptism is incorporated into the service of Morning or Evening Prayer from the Book of Common Prayer. Morning or Evening Prayer in Common Worship are governed by the provisions of A Service of the Word.

Items marked with an asterisk (*) have alternative positions – see the commentary in the relevant Resource sections below, and the Notes that follow this outline, for details.

The Sermon is placed in the position allowed for in permitted variations to the Book of Common Prayer. The notes and structure for a baptism service suggest a more appropriate position would be following the second reading.

¶ Introduction

[Thanksgiving Prayer for a Child – *optional*]
Introduction to Baptism

¶ Morning or Evening Prayer – Liturgy of the Word

Versicles (and *Venite* at MP)
Psalm(s)
OT Reading
Canticle
NT Reading

¶ The Liturgy of Baptism

Presentation of the Candidates *
The Decision
Signing with the Cross *
Prayer over the Water
Profession of Faith
Baptism
Commission *
The Welcome
[The Peace – *optional*]

¶ **Morning or Evening Prayer – *continues***

Canticle (MP *Benedictus* / EP *Nunc dimittis*)
Prayers *[possibly including Intercessions from Holy Baptism]*
Sermon *

¶ **The Sending Out**

The Blessing
Giving of a Lighted Candle *
The Dismissal

Notes

When appropriate, the service of Morning Prayer or Evening Prayer may be abbreviated. The Prayers of Penitence may be omitted, and the Creed is omitted, being replaced by one of the interrogatory forms provided in the service for Holy Baptism.

The service follows this order:

¶ The introduction to the service. This may include:
>Thanksgiving Prayer for a Child,
>Introduction
>Presentation of the Candidates

¶ Morning or Evening Prayer to the end of the second reading

¶ The Liturgy of Baptism, omitting the Presentation of the Candidates, if used earlier, and the Prayers of Intercession. The Peace may also be omitted.

¶ Morning or Evening Prayer from the canticle after the second reading, omitting the Apostles' Creed

¶ At the prayers, appropriate intercessions from the service for Holy Baptism may be used.

¶ The service concludes with the Sending Out.

The Notes to the service for Holy Baptism (pages 162–166) apply to the Thanksgiving Prayer for a Child, the Liturgy of Baptism and the Sending Out.

RESOURCE
SECTION

Resource Section

Introduction to the Resource Section

This section follows the 'default' structure for a service of Holy Baptism (Structure 1), which includes Holy Communion. This is not the only pattern possible, and different options are highlighted in the commentary material for each item (where relevant).

Each individual item (or group of items, if the whole group needs to be used as a single item) is given a reference code. This enables it to be identified clearly, and used for searching in the online material.

Liturgical material is found on the right hand page; the left hand page includes commentary, explanatory material, and guidance for using the liturgical material.

Sometimes the items within a section are alternatives (for instance, Section G The Decision); sometimes more than one of the items may be chosen (for instance, Section B Prayer of Thanksgiving). The explanatory material will make this clear.

A Greeting

The Greeting

The greeting given here is the standard greeting for a service of Holy Baptism from *Common Worship*, which is intended to be followed by more informal words of welcome and general introduction.

The Greeting may be followed by a brief introduction to baptism itself, and some scripted versions of this are provided in Section C.

In some contexts, other forms of greeting will be normal, especially if the service includes Holy Communion. This might include the Trinitarian ascription ('In the name of the Father, and of the Son and of the Holy Spirit. Amen.') and a simple 'The Lord be with you...', or the greeting 'Grace, mercy and peace from God our Father...' and in Eastertide, the Easter acclamation ('Alleluia. Christ is risen...') (see the *Common Worship* main volume, page 167).

A Service of the Word with Holy Baptism gives more open guidance: 'The minister welcomes the people with a liturgical Greeting.' This could include any of the above, other options from *New Patterns for Worship* Section A, or something that is particularly appropriate to the local context.

Greeting

The president says

The grace of our Lord Jesus Christ,
the love of God
and the fellowship of the Holy Spirit
be with you all
and also with you.   **A***1*

Words of welcome or introduction may be said.

B Prayer of Thanksgiving (and material from the service of Thanksgiving for the Gift of a Child)

This section contains optional material. Its use will depend on context and circumstances.

Thanksgiving Prayer for a Child

This extra prayer (B2) may be used where it is appropriate to express thanksgiving for a child who is going to be baptized later in the service. This is not intended to preclude the use of a separate service of Thanksgiving for the Gift of a Child. The introduction to the prayer (B1) could be used as printed or adapted as appropriate.

See below in this section for ways to incorporate elements from the full service of Thanksgiving for the Gift of a Child into a baptism service, where this is pastorally helpful.

Prayer of Thanksgiving

Introduction to the Thanksgiving Prayer

We rejoice today with *the family of N and N*
as *they* thank God for the gift of life
and bring *their children* for baptism.   **B** *1*

Thanksgiving Prayer for a Child

God our Creator,
we thank you for the wonder of new life
and for the mystery of human love.
We give thanks for all whose support and skill
surround and sustain the beginning of life.
As Jesus knew love and discipline within a human family,
may *these children* grow in strength and wisdom.
As Mary knew the joys and pains of motherhood,
give *these parents* your sustaining grace and love;
through Jesus Christ our Lord.
Amen.   **B** *2*

Material from the service of Thanksgiving for the Gift of a Child

Thanksgiving for the Gift of a Child is a separate service within *Common Worship*, designed for use after the birth or adoption of a child.

Parts of it are reproduced here for situations when thanksgiving is being incorporated as a significant element within a baptism service. This might simply be because parents are especially grateful to God for their child (perhaps because of particular pastoral circumstances), and wish to highlight that aspect more than the baptism service allows for (even with its optional Thanksgiving Prayer).

The material can also be particularly useful in situations where parents want to recognise people who are special to them and to their child, but who cannot be godparents because they are not baptized. This might include people of other faiths and those of no faith. The Thanksgiving service provides the opportunity to name and acknowledge these people as supporting friends.

Whatever the situation, if this material is being included in a baptism service, the most appropriate place to include it is early on. This means that the two ways of responding to God's grace (by giving thanks, and by seeking baptism) are kept distinct, and the celebrations of physical birth and spiritual birth are each given proper weight.

If any of the items (B3–B6) are used, they are used *instead* of items B1 and B2, not in addition to them. If this material is used, it makes sense to move from it straight to the Liturgy of the Word, and to save the Introduction to Baptism (Section C) until the Liturgy of Baptism, as part of the presentation of the candidate(s) for baptism.

Introduction to Thanksgiving for the Gift of a Child

The text at B3 combines the introduction to the Thanksgiving Prayer (B1) with an adapted form of the introduction to the service of Thanksgiving for the Gift of a Child. It does not have to be used verbatim, but some kind of brief introduction is important, so that everyone is clear what is going on in this part of the service.

Material from the service of Thanksgiving for the Gift of a Child

Introduction to Thanksgiving for the Gift of a Child

We rejoice today with *the family of N and N*
as *they* thank God for the gift of life
and bring *their children* for baptism.

In this part of the service
we are going to give thanks to God for *these children*,
and to support *their parents* in *their* responsibilities
with prayer and love.   **B***3*

Presentation for Thanksgiving

Because the baptism service also includes a Presentation, it is important that the more informal aspects (making sure the congregation can see the child, inviting the family to the front, allowing the family to say anything about why they have brought their child for Thanksgiving and Baptism, and so on) only take place once, at this earlier point. The later Presentation then becomes a more specific presentation of the candidate for *baptism*.

Depending on the circumstances, the supporting friends may be different from the godparents, or the same, or there may be a degree of overlap between the two groups.

Thanksgiving Prayer

The prayer of thanksgiving belongs with the questions to the parents and any supporting friends, because it is the immediate response to the desire to give thanks that has been expressed in the questions.

To simplify things, you could omit the later prayer for parents (B8) replacing the Thanksgiving Prayer here with the one at B2, which combines thanksgiving for the child with prayer for the parents.

Acknowledgement of the Child's Name

There is a powerful sense of connection between baptism and the 'naming' of a child, which persists even though the legal naming takes place at the registration of the child's birth. This is reflected in the use of the term 'christening' to mean 'naming' in all sorts of contexts which have nothing to do with Christian baptism.

The use of the child's name will be an important part of the baptism itself (and of the presentation of the child for baptism). However, if it is to be included as a significant feature in its own right, it makes sense to do so here, as this is the first point at which the child is officially presented to the congregation.

Presentation for Thanksgiving

Where parents wish to recognize the role of supporting friends it may be appropriate for them to stand with the parents at the thanksgiving. One of them may present the children to the minister, and informal words may be said.

The minister says to parents and any supporting friends

Do you receive these children as a gift from God?
We do.

Do you wish to give thanks to God and seek his blessing?
We do. B4

Thanksgiving Prayer

God our creator,
we thank you for the wonder of new life
and for the mystery of human love.
We thank you for all whose support and skill
surround and sustain the beginning of life.
We thank you that we are known to you by name
and loved by you from all eternity.
We thank you for Jesus Christ,
who has opened to us the way of love.
We praise you, Father, Son, and Holy Spirit.
Blessed be God for ever. B5

Acknowledgement of the Child's Name

The minister may say for each child

What name have you given this child?

A parent or supporting friend replies

His/her name is N. B6

Blessing of the Child

For some, the baptism itself will be an ample sign and instrument of God's grace and blessing for the child. Others may want to keep a clearer distinction between God's blessing (available for any child, whether baptized or not) and baptism as a particular sign of, and response to, God's grace.

Prayer for Parents

If this prayer is used here, make sure that any prayer for parents after the baptism focuses on their role in supporting the child's Christian faith and nurture.

Alternatively, this prayer could be saved for later, and incorporated into other prayers for parents after the baptism (see, for instance, item L5).

Giving of the Gospel

The Giving of the Gospel is a normal part of the service of Thanksgiving for the Gift of a Child, and helps to distinguish that service from baptism (at which a candle is often given).

In a baptism service which also incorporates Thanksgiving for the Gift of a Child, there is no reason why a Gospel and a candle should not both be presented, either separately, or perhaps together at the end of the service. If they are given together at the end of the service, a prayer like this could be used:

> 'Faithful God, walk with N every day of her/his life,
> with your presence
> and the guidance of your word to light her/his path.
> We ask it in the name of Jesus, the Light of the World. Amen.' **B9a**

Blessing of the Child

The minister may take the child.

As Jesus took children in his arms and blessed them,
so now we ask God's blessing on N.

Heavenly Father, we praise you for *his/her* birth;
surround *him/her* with your blessing
that *he/she* may know your love,
be protected from evil,
and know your goodness all *his/her* days.
Amen.   **B**7

Prayer for Parents

May God the Father of all bless *these parents*
and give *them* grace to love and care for *their children.*
May God give *them* wisdom, patience and faith,
help *them* to provide for *the children's* needs
and, by *their* example,
reveal the love and truth that are in Jesus Christ.
Amen.   **B**8

Giving of the Gospel

A copy of a Gospel is presented, with these words

Receive this book.
It is the good news of God's love.
Take it as your guide.   **B**9

Pledge by Supporting Friends

The pledges made by supporting friends in a Thanksgiving service are pledges to support the child and her/his family, rather than to a specifically Christian upbringing and connection with the Church. This is what makes them particularly helpful when parents want to recognize people who have already been special to them and who will be there for them in the years to come, but who (for whatever reason) cannot commit to leading by example in the child's specifically *Christian* upbringing.

This does not mean that supporting friends *cannot* be baptized and committed Christians – it simply means that they do not necessarily *have* to be. Other canonical constraints that apply to godparents (how many, which sex they are) also do not apply to supporting friends, giving a further degree of flexibility.

The pledge provided here is from the *Common Worship* Thanksgiving Service, but additional or alternative forms that connect with the particular pastoral situation could be used instead. The second question, addressed to the wider family and friends of the child, could equally well be answered by the whole congregation if appropriate.

Prayer by Parents or Congregation

This prayer makes a good way to round off this part of the service, before moving into the Liturgy of the Word. It would work beautifully as a prayer said by parents (perhaps with the supporting friends), but in contexts where the whole congregation know the child, it could be used as a congregational prayer. Another alternative would be for the minister to say the prayer on behalf of the parents.

A simple pattern

One way to incorporate elements of this material into a baptism service in a short and simple way, is to use the following items in this order:

B3; B4; B2; B7; B10; B9.

The Giving of the Gospel at the end of this would then lead neatly into the Liturgy of the Word.

Pledge by Supporting Friends

The minister may address the supporting friends and say

Will you do all that you can to help and support N and N in the bringing up of N?
With the help of God, we will.

The minister may address the wider family and friends and say

Will you do all that you can to help and support this family?
With the help of God, we will.   **B***10*

Prayer by Parents or Congregation

This prayer may be said by the parents or by the whole congregation

**God our creator,
we thank you for the gift of *these children*,
entrusted to our care.
May we be patient and understanding,
ready to guide and to forgive,
so that through our love
they may come to know your love;
through Jesus Christ our Lord. Amen.**   **B***11*

C Introductions to Baptism

This material is specifically about introducing and explaining baptism – it is not the more general welcome and introduction to the whole service, which will have come earlier.

The Pastoral Introduction

The Pastoral Introduction is intended as something to be printed and read individually by congregation members before the service begins, not read out loud in full.

It is not a mandatory text, and parishes may use or adapt it, or produce their own version, if they wish to include it in any locally produced order of service or to make it available on screen before the service begins.

However, ideas from this Pastoral Introduction might be adapted and used by the minister as part of a more informal spoken introduction to baptism and its meaning.

Pastoral Introduction

This may be read by those present before the service begins.

Baptism marks the beginning of a journey with God which continues for the rest of our lives, the first step in response to God's love. For all involved, particularly the candidates but also parents, godparents and sponsors, it is a joyful moment when we rejoice in what God has done for us in Christ, making serious promises and declaring the faith. The wider community of the local church and friends welcome the new Christian, promising support and prayer for the future. Hearing and doing these things provides an opportunity to remember our own baptism and reflect on the progress made on that journey, which is now to be shared with this new member of the Church.

The service paints many vivid pictures of what happens on the Christian way. There is the sign of the cross, the badge of faith in the Christian journey, which reminds us of Christ's death for us. Our 'drowning' in the water of baptism, where we believe we die to sin and are raised to new life, unites us to Christ's dying and rising, a picture that can be brought home vividly by the way the baptism is administered. Water is also a sign of new life, as we are born again by water and the Spirit. This reminds us of Jesus' baptism. And as a sign of that new life, there may be a lighted candle, a picture of the light of Christ conquering the darkness of evil. Everyone who is baptized walks in that light for the rest of their lives.

As you pray for the candidates, picture them with yourself and the whole Church throughout the ages, journeying into the fullness of God's love.

Jesus said, 'I came that they may have life, and have it abundantly.'

John 10.10

C1

Spoken introductions to baptism

Because these introductions are specifically about baptism, it is not appropriate to use them immediately before the Thanksgiving Prayer for a Child, or before material from the Thanksgiving for the Gift of a Child service. If any of that material is used, it should come first, before this introduction.

None of the introductions provided here are compulsory in this form – other words can be used, and these could be based on the forms provided, or more locally adapted, or more informal and extempore.

Special forms of introduction that relate to particular seasons are provided, but these are not compulsory. Equally, they are not restricted to the particular seasons indicated, but could be used at any time.

If the service includes Holy Communion, the Gloria in Excelsis may be used after the Introduction.

Introduction to Baptism – general

The president may use these or other words.

Our Lord Jesus Christ has told us
that to enter the kingdom of heaven
we must be born again of water and the Spirit,
and has given us baptism as the sign and seal of this new birth.
Here we are washed by the Holy Spirit and made clean.
Here we are clothed with Christ,
dying to sin that we may live his risen life.
As children of God, we have a new dignity
and God calls us to fullness of life.   **C**2

Introduction to Baptism – Epiphany/Baptism of Christ/Trinity

At our Lord's baptism in the river Jordan
God showed himself to all who have eyes to see
and ears to hear.
The Father spoke from heaven,
the Spirit descended as a dove
and Jesus was anointed with power from on high.
Here is the door of faith,
through which we enter the kingdom of heaven.
As children of God, we are adopted as his sons and daughters,
and called to proclaim the wonders of him
who called us out of darkness into his marvellous light.   **C**3

Introduction to Baptism – Easter/Pentecost

God raised Jesus Christ from the dead
and sent the Holy Spirit to recall the whole world to himself.
In baptism we die to sin and rise to newness of life in Christ.
Here we find rebirth in the Spirit,
and set our minds on his heavenly gifts.
As children of God, we are continually created anew,
as we walk the path of faith,
and feed on the forgiveness of his healing grace. **C4**

Introduction to Baptism – All Saints'/Advent

In baptism, God calls us to be his friends
and to make us holy in his Son Jesus Christ.
On this journey of faith we have no abiding city,
for we have the promise of the heavenly Jerusalem,
where the whole creation
is brought to a new birth in the Holy Spirit.
Here we are united in the company of all the faithful,
and we look for the coming of the eternal kingdom.
As children of God, we look through this passing age
for the signs of the dawn of everlasting glory. **C5**

D Collects

The normal collect to use on a Sunday is the Collect of the Day, but the text provided at D1 gives a collect that is more focused on baptism itself. This may be more appropriate to use when baptism is the predominant element of the service.

Other collect prayers that also pick up baptismal themes, but with a specific seasonal emphasis, are also provided (D2, D3, and D4).

The rubric reminds presiders that the Collect is intended to 'collect up' the prayers of all those present, so it is appropriately introduced with an invitation to pray and a generous silence to allow for people to pray in their own hearts.

The Collect – general

*The president introduces a period of silent prayer with the words 'Let us pray'
or a more specific bidding.*

*Either the Collect of the Day, or this Collect is said. Seasonal Collects are
also provided.*

Heavenly Father,
by the power of your Holy Spirit
you give your faithful people new life in the water of baptism.
Guide and strengthen us by the same Spirit,
that we who are born again may serve you in faith and love,
and grow into the full stature of your Son, Jesus Christ,
who is alive and reigns with you
in the unity of the Holy Spirit
now and for ever.
Amen.   **D** 1

Collects – seasonal alternatives

For most Sundays, the Collect of the Day would normally be used, especially in and around the key seasons of Christmas and Easter (that is, on Sundays between the First Sunday of Advent and the Feast of the Presentation of Christ, and between the First Sunday of Lent and Trinity Sunday).

However, the collects provided in the baptism service itself (D1), and the seasonal alternatives, can be used if appropriate, even when the normal Sunday readings from the lectionary are used.

As with the other seasonal material, the seasonal collects are not compulsory in these seasons, nor are they restricted to the season indicated. They can be used on any occasion to meet pastoral circumstances.

Collect – Epiphany/Baptism of Christ/Trinity

Lord of all time and eternity,
you opened heaven's gate and revealed yourself as Father
by the voice that called Jesus your beloved Son,
baptizing him, in the power of the Spirit:
reveal yourself to us now, to claim us as your children,
and so complete the heavenly work of our rebirth
in the waters of the new creation;
through Jesus Christ your Son our Lord,
who is alive and reigns with you, in the unity of the Holy Spirit,
one God, now and for ever.
Amen.   **D**2

Collect – Easter/Pentecost

Father of our Lord Jesus Christ,
from whose wounded side flowed life for the world:
raise your people from sin and death
and build them as living stones
into the spiritual temple of your Church;
through Jesus Christ your Son our Lord,
who lives and reigns with you in the unity of the Holy Spirit,
one God, world without end.
Amen.   **D**3

Collect – All Saints'/Advent

Almighty Father,
you have made us heirs through hope of your everlasting kingdom,
and in the waters of baptism you have promised
a measure of grace overflowing to all eternity.
Take our sins and guilt away,
and so inflame us with the life of your Spirit
that we may know your favour and goodness towards us,
and walk in newness of life, both now and for ever;
through Jesus Christ your Son our Lord,
who is alive and reigns with you, in the unity of the Holy Spirit,
one God, now and for ever.
Amen.   **D**4

E Scripture readings and lectionary options

For most Sundays, the lectionary readings for the day should normally be used, especially in those Sundays around the key seasons of Christmas and Easter (that is, between the First Sunday of Advent and the Feast of the Presentation of Christ, and between the first Sunday of Lent and Trinity Sunday). However, alternative sets of readings are provided (see below in this section), and these may be more appropriate to use, even within those key seasons, particularly where baptism is the predominant element in the service.

A general set of readings picks up on themes of baptism itself, and seasonal alternatives provide the opportunity to connect baptism with the emphases of the liturgical calendar.

Readings for Baptism

The rubrics and texts on the facing page are taken from the *Common Worship* baptism service. The notes make clear that for non-eucharistic services there need only be one reading, and that this should normally to be from one of the Gospels. The way this is introduced and responded to need not follow the texts on the facing page here. A Service of the Word provides more options and flexibility for how this might happen.

Sermon

There should always be a sermon at any baptism service. The preacher might include themes from the Commission, in which case the Commission can be omitted as a separate item.

Readings

The readings of the day are normally used on Sundays, Principal Feasts, other Principal Holy Days and Festivals. For other occasions, see pages 57–61.

Either one or two readings from Scripture may precede the Gospel reading.

At the end of each the reader may say

This is the word of the Lord.
Thanks be to God.

The psalm or canticle follows the first reading; other hymns and songs may be used between the readings.

E 1

Gospel Reading

An acclamation may herald the Gospel reading.

When the Gospel is announced the reader says

Hear the Gospel of our Lord Jesus Christ according to N.
Glory to you, O Lord.

At the end

This is the Gospel of the Lord.
Praise to you, O Christ.

E2

Sermon

Bible readings and psalms – general

Though the lectionary readings for the day are the normal starting point for a baptism service on a Sunday or Principal Feast, Holy Day or Festival, these alternative sets of readings are provided for situations where baptism is the predominant element of the service and the readings of the day are less appropriate. They would also be useful when (for pastoral reasons) the baptism is not taking place on a Sunday, Principal Feast, Holy Day or Festival.

Bible readings at Baptism – general

Old Testament	Psalm	New Testament	Gospel
Isaiah 43.1-7	Psalm 66.4-11	Romans 5.6-11	Mark 1.1-11 (9-11)
Genesis 17.1-8 or 22.15-18	Psalm 89.21, 22,25-29	Galatians 3.27 – 4.7	John 15.1-11
2 Kings 5.1-15a	Psalm 51.1-7	Titus 3.3-7	John 3.1-8
Genesis 7.1,7-16	Psalm 46.1-7	1 Peter 3.18-22	Matthew 28.16-20

Bible readings and psalms – seasonal

Though the lectionary readings for the day are the starting point for a baptism service on a Sunday or Principal Feast, Holy Day or Festival, these alternative sets of readings are provided for situations where baptism is the predominant element of the service and the readings of the day are less appropriate. They would also be useful when (for pastoral reasons) the baptism is not taking place on a Sunday, Principal Feast, Holy Day or Festival. They provide the opportunity to connect baptism with the emphases of the liturgical calendar.

Gospel acclamations

The Gospel acclamations (which are not compulsory) are from *Common Worship: Times and Seasons*, and pick up the themes of the different seasons, while also connecting with baptismal themes.

Bible readings at Baptism – Epiphany/Baptism of Christ/Trinity

Old Testament	Psalm	New Testament	Gospel
Exodus 33.12-20 or Isaiah 9.2,3,6,7	Psalm 67	2 Corinthians 3.12 – 4 6	John 1.14-18
Isaiah 42.5-8	Psalm 146.4-9	Acts 9.1-20 or 10-20	Luke 3.15-17,21,22
Isaiah 63.15,16 64.1-4	Psalm 50.1-6	1 Corinthians 10.1-4	Mark 1.1-11

Gospel Acclamation

Alleluia, alleluia.
This is my Son, the Beloved,
with whom I am well pleased.   *Matthew 3.17*
Alleluia.   **E**3

Bible readings at Baptism – Easter/Pentecost

Old Testament	Psalm	New Testament	Gospel
Ezekiel 37.1-14	Psalm 118.19-24	Romans 6.3-11	Matthew 28.16-20
Ezekiel 36.24-28	Psalm 51.7-14	Titus 3.3-7	John 20.19-23
Ezekiel 47.1-12	Psalm 46.1-7	Revelation 22.1-5	John 7.37-39

Gospel Acclamation

Alleluia, alleluia.
I am the first and the last, says the Lord, and the living one;
I was dead, and behold I am alive for evermore.   *cf Revelation 1.17,18*
Alleluia.   **E**4

Bible readings at Baptism – All Saints'/Advent

Old Testament	Psalm	New Testament	Gospel
Exodus 19.3-8	Psalm 98.1-4	Revelation 5.6-10	Matthew 28.16-20
Isaiah 44.1-5	Psalm 63.1-7	Hebrews 11.32 – 12.2	Matthew 5.1-12 *or* 1-16
Hosea 14.4-8	Psalm 92.10-15	1 Peter 2.4-10	John 15.1-11

Gospel Acclamation (All Saints' Day)

Alleluia, alleluia.

You are a chosen race, a royal priesthood,

a holy nation, God's own people,

called out of darkness into his marvellous light.   *1 Peter 2.9*

Alleluia.   **E**5

F The Presentation of the Candidates

The Presentation of the Candidates is placed by default in *Common Worship*, at the beginning of the Liturgy of Baptism, but it can instead come in the opening section of the service. If placed in this earlier position, it would come before the Gloria in Excelsis (if used) and the Collect.

Option 1

This is the material from the original *Common Worship* services. Here it is divided into three items to indicate how to use it with different combinations of candidates.

1 If all the candidates **can answer for themselves**, only items F1 and F2 will be needed.

2 If all the candidates are all **infants** or **others unable to answer for themselves**, only items F2 and F3 will be needed.

3 If the candidates include **some who can answer for themselves and some who cannot**, all three items F1, F2 and F3 will be needed, in that order, each used for the respective candidates.

4 If the candidates include **young children who nonetheless are able to speak for themselves**, it may be pastorally appropriate for them to answer for themselves *and* then the parents and godparents also be asked the questions at item F3.

Option 2, below, takes a different approach, and gives two alternative sets of words for adult or infant candidates. This means that if you have a mixture of candidates at one service, the two options work differently.

The giving of testimony

See the guidance overleaf, under Option 2, for more on what is envisaged by 'testimony'.

Presentation – Option 1

The candidates may be presented to the congregation. Where appropriate, they may be presented by their godparents or sponsors.

For candidates able to answer for themselves

The president asks those candidates for baptism who are able to answer for themselves

Do you wish to be baptized?
I do.

Testimony by the candidate(s) may follow.　　　　　　　　　　　　　　**F1**

For all candidates

The president addresses the whole congregation

Faith is the gift of God to his people.
In baptism the Lord is adding to our number
　those whom he is calling.
People of God, will you welcome *these children/candidates*
and uphold *them* in *their* new life in Christ?
With the help of God, we will.　　　　　　　　　　　　　　**F2**

For infant candidates

At the baptism of children, the president then says to the parents and godparents

Parents and godparents, the Church receives *these children* with joy.
Today we are trusting God for *their* growth in faith.
Will you pray for *them*, draw *them* by your example
into the community of faith and walk with *them* in the way of Christ?
With the help of God, we will.

In baptism *these children* begin *their* journey in faith.
You speak for *them* today.
Will you care for *them*, and help *them* to take *their* place
within the life and worship of Christ's Church?
With the help of God, we will.　　　　　　　　　　　　　　**F3**

Option 2

This is the material from the Additional Baptism Texts in Accessible Language.

Note that there are two separate items here:

- F4 – Material for use with **infants**.
- F5 – Material for use with **candidates who are able to answer for themselves**.

Simply choose the appropriate item to suit the candidates. If you have both adult and infant candidates, both items will be needed, including the two different sets of questions to the congregation about their support.

What is envisaged by 'testimony'?

The telling of the human story is an important part of baptism (see the section in the 'Introduction to Baptism in *Common Worship*' above, page 8). The intention of testimony in the baptism service is that, in some circumstances, individuals may value the opportunity to give a brief personal explanation of how they have come to faith. This does not necessarily imply one particular style of personal presentation. For instance, it could be done by means of a short interview (perhaps led by someone from the church's baptism preparation team, or the candidate's sponsor), or the candidate might write something that could be printed in full in any service sheet, and parts of it read out in the service.

It's important not to interrupt the flow of the service, or compete with the sermon, so aim to keep things focused and concise, whichever way the testimony is handled.

Presentation – Option 2

The candidates may be presented to the congregation. Where appropriate, they may be presented by their godparents or sponsors.

For infant candidates

The president addresses the whole congregation

Jesus said, 'Let the children come to me. Do not stop them'.
We thank God for *N and N* who *have* come to be baptized today.
Christ loves *them* and welcomes *them* into his Church.
So I ask you all:

Will you support *these children* as *they begin their* journey of faith?
We will.

Will you help *them* to live and grow within God's family?
We will.

The president then addresses the parents and godparents

God knows each of us by name and we are his.
Parents and godparents, you speak for *N and N* today.
Will you pray for *them*, and help *them* to follow Christ?
We will.   F4

For candidates able to answer for themselves

The president asks those candidates who are able to answer for themselves

Do you wish to be baptized?
I do.

Testimony by the candidate(s) may follow.

The president addresses the whole congregation

We thank God for *N and N* who *have* come to be baptized today.
Christ loves *them* and welcomes *them* into his Church.
Will you support *them* on *their* journey of faith?
We will.   F5

G The Decision

General comments

The large candle could be, but does not have to be, the Easter candle. Where it is used, and individual candles are going to be given to the newly baptized later in the service, these can be lit from the large candle.

By default, the Signing with the Cross follows directly after the Decision. If, instead, the signing is taking place immediately after the baptism itself, one of the concluding prayers from Section H (item H3 or H5) is still used to conclude the Decision.

The Decision – Option 1

In Option 1, between the first three questions and the second three questions, there could be movement or a turning to indicate a shift between those things we turn away from and those things we turn towards. For instance, the candidates (and parents and godparents) might turn towards the Easter candle, or turn to face the font, ready to move towards it later, or they might turn from West to East.

Another way to signal this shift between the first three and second three questions might be to split the opening sentences. 'In baptism, God calls us out of darkness into his marvellous light' could precede the first three questions. 'To follow Christ means dying to sin and rising to new life with him' could be moved to precede the second three questions. This would fall within the provision in Canon B5 for 'variations which are not of substantial importance' to be made at the discretion of the minister.

For further ideas, see the comments below for Option 2.

The Decision – Option 1

A large candle may be lit.

The president addresses the candidates directly, or through their parents, godparents and sponsors

In baptism, God calls us out of darkness into his marvellous light.
To follow Christ means dying to sin and rising to new life with him.

Therefore I ask:

Do you reject the devil and all rebellion against God?
I reject them.

Do you renounce the deceit and corruption of evil?
I renounce them.

Do you repent of the sins that separate us from God and neighbour?
I repent of them.

Do you turn to Christ as Saviour?
I turn to Christ.

Do you submit to Christ as Lord?
I submit to Christ.

Do you come to Christ, the way, the truth and the life?
I come to Christ.   **G1**

The Decision – Option 2

This is the material from the Additional Baptism Texts in Accessible Language. The candidates' response to each question is deliberately kept the same, making it easier for them to be released from a text (either in print or on screen) and to engage with the action.

There are two pairs of questions. Between them is the idea of turning around – conversion – and this could be expressed by some action.

- The first pair of questions represents a movement away from sin and evil – all that keeps us apart from God.
- The second pair represents a turning towards newness of life and faith in Christ. This could be expressed through a physical movement or turning.

If there is to be an actual turning, or a movement from one place to another, the details will need to take into account the layout of the church. The first pair of questions might typically be answered facing away from the East or standing at a distance from any of the key symbols in the church. The second pair could then take place after turning or moving towards a symbolic location of new life in the risen Christ, such as the font, holy table, a cross or the Easter candle. (Ministers will need to think carefully about where they themselves stand at this point, so that the symbolic turning does not appear as a turning towards the minister.)

The 'large candle' (usually the Easter candle) is not specifically mentioned, but it could form part of the movement or action. It could be lit before the Decision is used, as indicated in Options 1 and 3, or perhaps lit between the two pairs of questions, as the candidates, parents, godparents and sponsors turn towards it.

The Decision – Option 2

The president addresses the candidates directly, or through their parents, godparents and sponsors

We all wander far from God and lose our way:
Christ comes to find us and welcomes us home.
In baptism we respond to his call.

Therefore I ask:

Do you turn away from sin?
I do.
Do you reject evil?
I do.

The candidates, together with their parents, godparents and sponsors, may turn at this point.

Do you turn to Christ as Saviour?
I do.
Do you trust in him as Lord?
I do. **G**2

The Decision – Option 3

Option 3 is the material provided in the original *Common Worship* material, for use 'where there are strong pastoral reasons'.

No introductory sentence is specifically provided in *Common Worship*, but in order to make sense of the 'Therefore I ask', something needs to be said. The forms from Option 1 or Option 2 have been printed here, and one of these could be used, or some other suitable words.

The Decision – Option 3

A large candle may be lit.

The president addresses the candidates directly, or through their parents, godparents and sponsors

[The questions should be introduced using this

In baptism, God calls us out of darkness into his marvellous light.
To follow Christ means dying to sin and rising to new life with him.

or this

We all wander far from God and lose our way:
Christ comes to find us and welcomes us home.
In baptism we respond to his call.

or some other suitable form of words.]

Therefore I ask:

Do you turn to Christ?
I turn to Christ.

Do you repent of your sins?
I repent of my sins.

Do you renounce evil?
I renounce evil.

G3

H The Signing with the Cross

General points about the Signing

The minister traces the sign of the cross on the candidate's forehead; this may be done using olive oil (sometimes called the oil of baptism or the oil of catechumens). For more about the use of oil, see the Introduction to Baptism in *Common Worship* above, pages 10–11.

Parents, godparents and sponsors may also be invited to sign the candidate (with the oil, if desired).

If there are several candidates, items H2 and H3 only need to be used once, when all the candidates have been signed.

Origins

The roots of the signing (in its default position after the Decision) lie in the enrolment of catechumens at the beginning of a period of preparation for baptism, a practice that has been renewed in some parishes. There is rich biblical symbolism associated with anointing: it is an image of cleansing, blessing, consecration to God's purpose, and of preparation for athletic contest which is itself an image of 'running the race' of the Christian life (see 1 Samuel 16.13; Psalms 23.5; 45.7; 133.2). Many parishes use oil that has been blessed by the Bishop (though this is not compulsory), which is a reminder that each individual baptism is also an act of the whole Church.

The Signing – Option 1

This is the original *Common Worship* material.

Alternative position

The default place for the Signing with the Cross is here, after the Decision. The alternative is to do it immediately after the baptism itself. In that case, it should accompany the prayer for God's grace and renewal by the Spirit, which follows baptism, rather than using the words provided in this section.

If no signing takes place in this section after the Decision, the words of items H1 and H2 are omitted ('Christ claims you...' and, 'Do not be ashamed ...'). Item H3 (the prayer, 'May almighty God deliver you ...') is, however, still used to conclude the Decision.

The Signing – Option 1

The president or another minister makes the sign of the cross on the forehead of each candidate, saying

Christ claims you for his own.
Receive the sign of his cross.

The president may invite parents, godparents and sponsors to sign the candidates with the cross.   **H**1

When all the candidates have been signed, the president says

Do not be ashamed to confess the faith of Christ crucified.
Fight valiantly as a disciple of Christ
against sin, the world and the devil,
and remain faithful to Christ to the end of your life.   **H2**

May almighty God deliver you from the powers of darkness,
restore in you the image of his glory,
and lead you in the light and obedience of Christ.
Amen.   **H3**

The Signing – Option 2

This is the material from the Additional Baptism Texts in Accessible Language.

The sense of needing persistence and courage to follow Christ is retained, but without the more militaristic (and archaic) language of 'fighting valiantly' that Option 1 uses.

Alternative position

The default place for the Signing with the Cross is after the Decision. The alternative is to do it immediately after the baptism itself. In that case, it should accompany the prayer for God's grace and renewal by the Spirit, which follows baptism, rather than using the words provided in this section.

If no signing takes place in this section after the Decision, the words of items H1 and H4 are omitted ('Christ claims you...' and, 'Do not be ashamed ...'). Item H5 (the prayer, 'May almighty God deliver you ...') is, however, still used to conclude the Decision.

The Signing – Option 2

*The president or another minister makes the sign of the cross on the forehead of
each candidate, saying*

Christ claims you for his own.
Receive the sign of his cross.

*The president may invite parents, godparents and sponsors
to sign the candidates with the cross.*   **H***1*

When all the candidates have been signed, the president says

Do not be ashamed of Christ.
You are his for ever.
**Stand bravely with him
against all the powers of evil,
and remain faithful to Christ to the end of your life.**   **H4**

May almighty God deliver you from the powers of darkness,
and lead you in the light and obedience of Christ.
Amen.   **H5**

I Prayer over the Water

On the way to the font

The *Common Worship* rubric says that, 'A canticle, psalm, hymn or litany may be used'. A selection of these is reproduced in this volume at pages 150–157 (items T1 to T6).

Introductory dialogue

The opening dialogue between president and congregation (item I1) can be used at the start of any of the Prayers over the Water in this section.

Prayers over the Water

Given that water is essential to the performance of a baptism and that the symbolism of water is central to its meaning, it is worth drawing attention to the water. It could, for instance, be poured into the font from a jug, visibly and audibly, possibly by a godparent, before the Prayer over the Water. If the baptism is taking place in a baptismal pool it will clearly need to be in place before the service starts, but the minister might still scoop up some of the water with a hand as they pray, or extra water might be added.

Prayers over the Water are not entirely specific to the individual being baptized so they refer, in the plural, to 'those who are washed in this water' and 'those who are baptized in it [this water]'. There is no need to alter those words when only one individual is being baptized.

Choosing a Prayer

The individual prayers (items I2 to I9) are alternatives – simply choose the one most appropriate to the context of the service.

Prayer over the Water – Option 1 (item I2)

This is the default prayer from *Common Worship*.

Prayer over the Water – Introductory dialogue

The ministers and candidates gather at the baptismal font.

The president stands before the water of baptism and says

Praise God who made heaven and earth,
who keeps his promise for ever.

Let us give thanks to the Lord our God.
It is right to give thanks and praise.

11

Prayer over the Water – Option 1

We thank you, almighty God, for the gift of water
to sustain, refresh and cleanse all life.
Over water the Holy Spirit moved in the beginning of creation.
Through water you led the children of Israel
from slavery in Egypt to freedom in the Promised Land.
In water your Son Jesus received the baptism of John
and was anointed by the Holy Spirit as the Messiah, the Christ,
to lead us from the death of sin to newness of life.

We thank you, Father, for the water of baptism.
In it we are buried with Christ in his death.
By it we share in his resurrection.
Through it we are reborn by the Holy Spirit.
Therefore, in joyful obedience to your Son,
we baptize into his fellowship those who come to him in faith.

Now sanctify this water that, by the power of your Holy Spirit,
they may be cleansed from sin and born again.
Renewed in your image, may they walk by the light of faith
and continue for ever in the risen life of Jesus Christ our Lord;
to whom with you and the Holy Spirit
be all honour and glory, now and for ever.
Amen.

12

Prayer over the Water – Option 2 (item I3)

This is the first of two prayers provided in the Additional Baptism Texts in Accessible Language material. It is designed to be short and to focus attention on two key baptismal images: the imagery of Moses leading the people to freedom through the Red Sea and Christ's passing through the deep waters of death, leading to prayer that the candidates may die and rise with him and find true freedom themselves.

Prayer over the Water – Option 3 (item I4)

This is the second prayer from the *Additional Baptism Texts in Accessible Language* material. It focuses on Christ's baptism when the Spirit came on him and he was revealed as God's beloved Son, leading to prayer that the candidates may be cleansed and filled with the Spirit so that they too may know they are loved as God's children.

Prayer over the Water – Option 2

Loving Father,
we thank you for your servant Moses,
who led your people through the waters of the Red Sea
to freedom in the Promised Land.
We thank you for your Son Jesus,
who has passed through the deep waters of death
and opened for all the way of salvation.
Now send your Spirit,
that those who are washed in this water
may die with Christ and rise with him,
to find true freedom as your children,
alive in Christ for ever.
Amen.   13

Prayer over the Water – Option 3

We praise you, loving Father,
for the gift of your Son Jesus.
He was baptized in the River Jordan,
where your Spirit came upon him
and revealed him as the Son you love.
He sent his followers
to baptize all who turn to him.
Now, Father, we ask you to bless this water,
that those who are baptized in it
may be cleansed in the water of life,
and, filled with your Spirit,
may know that they are loved as your children,
safe in Christ for ever.
Amen.   14

Prayer over the Water – Option 4 (item I5)

This prayer, from the original *Common Worship* material, is designed to give a voice to the congregation, and so engage them more actively in this key prayer.

The idea is that the refrain '**Lord of life, renew your creation**' could be said or sung by everyone.

To make it easier to join in without having to focus on reading the words, the first phrase, *'Lord of life'* (italicized) could be said or sung by a deacon, a cantor, or another minister as a regular cue line, with the congregation responding with, '**renew your creation**'.

Prayer over the Water – Option 4: responsive

We thank you, almighty God, for the gift of water
to sustain, refresh and cleanse all life.
Over water the Holy Spirit moved in the beginning of creation.
Through water you led the children of Israel
from slavery in Egypt to freedom in the Promised Land.
In water your Son Jesus received the baptism of John
and was anointed by the Holy Spirit as the Messiah, the Christ,
to lead us from the death of sin to newness of life.
Lord of life,
renew your creation.

We thank you, Father, for the water of baptism.
In it we are buried with Christ in his death.
By it we share in his resurrection.
Through it we are reborn by the Holy Spirit.
Therefore, in joyful obedience to your Son,
we baptize into his fellowship those who come to him in faith.
Lord of life,
renew your creation.

Now sanctify this water that, by the power of your Holy Spirit,
they may be cleansed from sin and born again.
Renewed in your image, may they walk by the light of faith
and continue for ever in the risen life of Jesus Christ our Lord;
to whom with you and the Holy Spirit
be all honour and glory, now and for ever. Amen.
Lord of life,
renew your creation.   15

Prayer over the Water – Option 5 (item I6)

This is the first of a series of seasonal prayers over the water provided in *Common Worship*. Though the headings indicate seasons in which they might be particularly appropriate, they can be used on any occasion.

These prayers represent a conscious broadening of baptismal images beyond those associated solely with the Easter themes of dying and rising with Christ. Although there is a strong Western tradition of Paschal emphasis, older Western rites retained a broader and more complex range of images, including that of a new birth by water and the Spirit within the new creation.

Prayer over the Water – Option 5: seasonal (Epiphany/Baptism of Christ/Trinity)

Father, we give you thanks and praise
for your gift of water in creation;
for your Spirit, sweeping over the waters,
bringing light and life;
for your Son Jesus Christ our Lord,
baptized in the river Jordan.

We bless you for your new creation,
brought to birth by water and the Spirit,
and for your grace bestowed upon us your children,
washing away our sins.

May your holy and life-giving Spirit
move upon these waters.
Restore through them the beauty of your creation,
and bring those who are baptized
to new birth in the family of your Church.

Drown sin in the waters of judgement,
anoint your children with power from on high,
and make them one with Christ
in the freedom of your kingdom.
For all might, majesty, dominion and power are yours,
now and for ever.
Alleluia. Amen.   16

Prayer over the Water – Option 6 (item I7)

This takes the material from Option 5, and turns it into a responsorial prayer shaped as a dialogue between presider and congregation.

Note that the response changes halfway through the prayer. To signal that this is coming, the president might need to change pace and tone at 'Father, accept our sacrifice of praise...' to signal the shift from praise to petition.

Prayer over the Water – Option 6: seasonal, responsive (Epiphany/Baptism of Christ/Trinity)

Father, for your gift of water in creation,
we give you thanks and praise.

For your Spirit, sweeping over the waters, bringing light and life,
we give you thanks and praise.

For your Son Jesus Christ our Lord, baptized in the river Jordan,
we give you thanks and praise.

For your new creation, brought to birth by water and the Spirit,
we give you thanks and praise.

For your grace bestowed upon us your children,
washing away our sins,
we give you thanks and praise.

Father, accept our sacrifice of praise;
may your holy and life-giving Spirit move upon these waters.
Lord, receive our prayer.

Restore through them the beauty of your creation,
and bring those who are baptized
to new birth in the family of your Church.
Lord, receive our prayer.

Drown sin in the waters of judgement,
anoint your children with power from on high,
and make them one with Christ in the freedom of your kingdom.
Lord, receive our prayer.

For all might, majesty, dominion and power are yours,
now and for ever.
Alleluia. Amen.   17

Prayer over the Water – Option 7 (item I8)

This seasonal prayer brings out themes particularly appropriate in the season of Easter, or at Pentecost, but it can be used at any other time.

The bracketed refrain '*Saving God,* **give us life**' is optional. If it is used, it could be said or sung by everyone.

To make it easier to join in without having to focus on reading the words, the first phrase, '*Saving God*' (italicized) could be said or sung by a deacon, a cantor, or another minister as a regular cue line, with the congregation responding with, '**give us life**'.

Prayer over the Water – Option 7: seasonal, responsive (Easter/Pentecost)

Almighty God, whose Son Jesus Christ
was baptized in the river Jordan,
we thank you for the gift of water
to cleanse us and revive us.
[*Saving God*,
give us life.]

We thank you that through the waters of the Red Sea
you led your people out of slavery
to freedom in the Promised Land.
[*Saving God*,
give us life.]

We thank you that through the deep waters of death
        you brought your Son,
and raised him to life in triumph.
[*Saving God*,
give us life.]

Bless this water, that your servants who are washed in it
may be made one with Christ in his death and in his resurrection,
to be cleansed and delivered from all sin.
[*Saving God*,
give us life.]

Send your Holy Spirit upon them,
bring them to new birth in the household of faith
and raise them with Christ to full and eternal life;
for all might, majesty, authority and power are yours,
now and for ever. Amen.
[*Saving God*,
give us life.]   18

Prayer over the Water – Option 8 (item I9)

This seasonal prayer brings out themes particularly appropriate in the season from All Saints' Day (or All Saints' Sunday) to Advent, but it can be used at any other time.

The bracketed refrain '*Hope of the saints,* **make known your glory'** is optional. If it is used, it could be said or sung by everyone.

To make it easier to join in without having to focus on reading the words, the first phrase, '*Hope of the saints*' (italicized) could be said or sung by a deacon, a cantor, or another minister as a regular cue line, with the congregation responding with, '**make known your glory'**.

Prayer over the Water – Option 8: seasonal, responsive (All Saints'/Advent)

Lord of the heavens,
we bless your name for all your servants
who have been a sign of your grace through the ages.
**[*Hope of the saints,*
make known your glory.]**

You delivered Noah from the waters of destruction;
you divided the waters of the sea, and by the hand of Moses
you led your people from slavery into the Promised Land.
**[*Hope of the saints,*
make known your glory.]**

You made a new covenant in the blood of your Son,
that all who confess his name may, by the Holy Spirit,
enter the covenant of grace,
receive a pledge of the kingdom of heaven,
and share in the divine nature.
**[*Hope of the saints,*
make known your glory.]**

Fill these waters, we pray, with the power of that same Spirit,
that all who enter them may be reborn
and rise from the grave to new life in Christ.
**[*Hope of the saints,*
make known your glory.]**

As the apostles and prophets, the confessors and martyrs,
faithfully served you in their generation,
may we be built into an eternal dwelling for you,
through Jesus Christ our Lord,
to whom with you and the Holy Spirit
be honour and glory, now and for ever. Amen.
**[*Hope of the saints,*
make known your glory.]**   19

J Profession of Faith

Profession of Faith

The Profession of Faith is not just for the candidates, but for the whole congregation. The candidates join with the Church in making clear the faith into which they will be baptized and which they share with Christians down the ages and round the world.

Option 1

The Apostles' Creed is the normal baptismal creed in the Western tradition. *Common Worship* provides it by default in this question and answer form.

The form of the question helps make it clear that these are not simply intellectual beliefs, but statements of trust in the persons of the Trinity.

Profession of Faith – Option 1: Apostles' Creed (responsorial)

The president addresses the congregation

Brothers and sisters, I ask you to profess
together with *these* candidates
the faith of the Church.

Do you believe and trust in God the Father?
**I believe in God, the Father almighty,
creator of heaven and earth.**

Do you believe and trust in his Son Jesus Christ?
**I believe in Jesus Christ, his only Son, our Lord,
who was conceived by the Holy Spirit,
born of the Virgin Mary, suffered under Pontius Pilate,
was crucified, died, and was buried;
he descended to the dead.
On the third day he rose again;
he ascended into heaven,
he is seated at the right hand of the Father,
and he will come to judge the living and the dead.**

Do you believe and trust in the Holy Spirit?
**I believe in the Holy Spirit,
the holy catholic Church,
the communion of saints,
the forgiveness of sins,
the resurrection of the body,
and the life everlasting.
Amen.** J1

Option 2

Common Worship provides this alternative form of Profession of Faith for use, 'Where there are strong pastoral reasons…'. It gives the longer, varying, text to the minister, and gives shorter repeated answers to the congregation, which can help people with visual impairment, or others for whom reading lots of words is difficult or slow.

When can this alternative form of Profession of Faith be used?

The rubric in *Common Worship* limits the use of this form (to situations in which there are 'strong pastoral reasons') out of a desire to honour the Anglican commitment (embodied in the 1888 Lambeth Quadrilateral) that the Apostles' Creed be regarded as the 'baptismal symbol', that is, the form of the public baptismal profession to which the Church is committed.

The alternative form is provided, therefore, not to avoid the rich complexity of Christian belief reflected in the Creed, but to simplify its form of expression and to ease the practicalities of reciting long texts together. Where possible, therefore, the Apostles' Creed should be preferred, as connecting us with a wider and longer tradition of expressing belief in the Holy Trinity. Where the alternative form is used in the service itself, it might be possible to use baptismal preparation as an opportunity to introduce the Creed as an expression of a long-held distillation of the Church's key beliefs, into which the candidate is being initiated.

Profession of Faith – Option 2: alternative form

The president says

Let us affirm,
together with *these* who *are* being baptized,
our common faith in Jesus Christ.

Do you believe and trust in God the Father,
source of all being and life,
the one for whom we exist?
I believe and trust in him.

Do you believe and trust in God the Son,
who took our human nature,
died for us and rose again?
I believe and trust in him.

Do you believe and trust in God the Holy Spirit,
who gives life to the people of God
and makes Christ known in the world?
I believe and trust in him.

This is the faith of the Church.
This is our faith.
We believe and trust in one God,
Father, Son and Holy Spirit.

J2

K Baptism

Administration of water

While a threefold dipping or pouring connects us with a very ancient tradition, and speaks naturally of the Trinitarian faith into which candidates are baptized, a single administration of water is also valid. This might be more practical, for instance, if an adult candidate is being submerged. The key thing is the use of the Trinitarian formula.

The president can delegate the actual administration of the water to 'another lawful minister' (see Note 12, page 164).

Amount of water

The Notes to *Common Worship* Holy Baptism encourage the use of 'a substantial amount of water', which should 'at least flow on the skin of the candidate' (see Note 12, page 164). This enhances the power and impact of the symbolism of baptism – entry into new life ought to look like something significant. It also addresses the questions raised in certain ecumenical discussions about the validity of Anglican baptisms where the candidates appear to be merely dabbed with water.

The encouragement to use significant amounts of water has further implications – a tiny plastic bowl holding the water (possibly inside a much larger font) both hinders the use of lots of water, and subverts the symbolism of baptism's significance.

Conditional Baptism

There is a special form of words to use if someone is unsure whether they have already been baptized or not (see Note 13, page 165):

> N, if you have not already been baptized,
> I baptize you in the name of the Father,
> and of the Son,
> and of the Holy Spirit. **Amen.**   **K2a**

Baptism

If the candidate(s) can answer for themselves, the president may say to each one

N, is this your faith?

Each candidate answers in their own words, or

This is my faith.   **K**1

The president or another minister dips each candidate in water, or pours water on them, saying

N, I baptize you in the name of the Father,
and of the Son,
and of the Holy Spirit.

Amen.   **K**2

Clothing (optional)

The explicit provision for clothing after baptism is provided for three reasons:

- There is often a practical need for some form of clothing to take place immediately after any baptism that involves immersion or submersion. There is scope for making something positive out of a practical necessity.

- There are some places where family traditions involving a christening gown for infant baptism are still strong. This gives an opportunity to build on an existing popular custom, particularly where infants are clothed in the christening gown after the water baptism, rather than from the start of the service.

- Accompanying the clothing with a spoken text drawn from the New Testament (Galatians 3.27) gives a vivid and memorable way to symbolize the biblical language about 'putting on' Christ.

The words are primarily an interpretive accompaniment to the action, so they should only be used where the action is going to be visible and significant.

If this optional provision feels appropriate, it can help the momentum of the service to be sustained in a context where the need for drying and clothing can easily give rise to a hiatus.

Where there are adult baptisms by immersion or submersion, the common Baptist tradition of offering a white towelling dressing gown to the newly baptized candidates could provide a suitable modern form of the ancient tradition of clothing.

Clothing

If the newly baptized are clothed with a white robe, a hymn or song may be used, and then a minister may say

You have been clothed with Christ.
As many as are baptized into Christ have put on Christ. **K3**

Signing with the Cross – alternative position

The Signing with the Cross normally takes place earlier in the service (after the Decision), but it can instead come here, immediately after baptism. The words accompanying the Signing in Section H should *not* be used in this later position.

Instead, the signing should follow the administration of water as a separate action that precedes or accompanies the Prayer for Grace and Renewal by the Spirit (item K4). This is important to avoid the common misunderstanding that thinks of baptism itself as making the sign of the cross using water.

The use of oil

Oil may be used for the Signing with the Cross in this alternative position, or as a supplementary anointing to accompany the prayer for grace and renewal by the Spirit. In either case, if oil is to be used in this position, it would normally be the oil of chrism (oil mixed with perfume or spices), rather than the oil of baptism (which is normally pure olive oil).

If oil is being used for the Signing with the Cross (in its alternative position) a simple cross shape is used.

If oil is being used as a supplementary anointing to accompany the prayer at item K4, it could take one of three possible forms:

- A simple pouring of oil on the crown of the candidate's head.

- A simple application of oil to the candidate's forehead.

- An application of oil to the forehead in the sign of a chi-rho (the first two letters of the Greek word for Christ), signifying Christos, the Anointed One. This would look like a diagonal cross with a letter 'P' superimposed on it, and avoids a repetition of the simple cross used after the Decision.

In each case, it is the oil which is the key symbol, and not the way it is applied.

For more about the use of oil, see the Introduction to Baptism in *Common Worship* above, pages 10–11.

Signing with the Cross
(alternative position)

If those who have been baptized were not signed with the cross immediately after the Decision, the president signs each one now.

Prayer for Grace and Renewal by the Spirit

The president says

May God, who has received you by baptism into his Church,
pour upon you the riches of his grace,
that within the company of Christ's pilgrim people
you may daily be renewed by his anointing Spirit,
and come to the inheritance of the saints in glory.

Amen.   **K**4

The president and those who have been baptized may return from the font.

Giving of a Lighted Candle – alternative position

The default position for the optional Giving of a Lighted Candle is at the conclusion of the service, where it acts as a symbol of mission.

Alternatively, it can take place here, after the baptism itself (following the Prayer for Grace and Renewal by the Spirit). If this is the case, make sure you give clear instructions about what to do with the candle after it has been lit. If it is to be blown out for safety reasons, it is important that this does not look like a symbolic action, extinguishing the light of Christ.

Giving of a Lighted Candle
(alternative position)

The president or another person may give each of the newly baptized
a lighted candle.

These may be lit from the candle used at the Decision.

When all the newly baptized have received a candle, the president says

God has delivered us from the dominion of darkness
and has given us a place with the saints in light.

You have received the light of Christ;
walk in this light all the days of your life.
**Shine as a light in the world
to the glory of God the Father.**   K5

L Commission

Option 1: infant candidates

This is the original *Common Worship* commission material for use with candidates who cannot answer for themselves. It is addressed primarily to the parents and godparents.

The text provided is meant to be a starting point – the rubric ('using these or similar words') is an encouragement to make sure that the actual form used is appropriate both to the candidates and to the context. It can be adapted or paraphrased instead if necessary, or similar material can be included in the sermon.

When there are candidates who can answer for themselves, the Commission material provided for them (Options 3 and 4) can be used instead (or in addition, if there is a mixture of candidates), or Option 3 can be used at the beginning of the Sending Out.

As it is structured here, with the final section in square brackets, this Commission ends with a link into prayer. This could be either a prayer for the parents (see item L5 below), or more general intercessions (which would include the parents).

If the service is structured so that the Commission leads directly into the Welcome (without the prayer for parents at item L5 and with the intercessions coming later), the last part of the Commission (in square brackets) will need to be omitted or adjusted accordingly.

Commission – Option 1: infant candidates

A minister addresses the congregation, parents and godparents, using these or similar words

We have brought *these children* to baptism knowing that Jesus died and rose again for *them* and trusting in the promise that God hears and answers prayer. We have prayed that in Jesus Christ *they* will know the forgiveness of *their* sins and the new life of the Spirit.

As *they* grow up, *they* will need the help and encouragement of the Christian community, so that *they* may learn to know God in public worship and private prayer, follow Jesus Christ in the life of faith, serve *their* neighbour after the example of Christ, and in due course come to confirmation.

As part of the Church of Christ, we all have a duty to support *them* by prayer, example and teaching. As *their* parents and godparents, you have the prime responsibility for guiding and helping *them* in *their* early years. This is a demanding task for which you will need the help and grace of God.

[Therefore let us now pray for grace in guiding *these children* in the way of faith.]

L/

Option 2: infant candidates

In place of the forms of Commission provided in *Common Worship,* alternatives are provided in the Additional Baptism Texts in Accessible Language.

That material makes even clearer that the minister (or other suitable person) should talk directly and simply in his or her own words to the parents, godparents and congregation, covering the topics listed in the bullet points.

Some ministers may find it helpful to speak from these bullet-points, but it is important to make the words flow and not to give the impression that a written text is simply being read out.

An example might go like this

'Parents and godparents, we are glad to have welcomed you here for the baptism of N *and* N. Today they have joined us on our Christian journey. Baptism unites us with Christ and to his whole Church, on earth and in heaven.

'Here, we'll do all that we can to ensure that there is a welcoming place for you. We will play our part in helping you guide these children along the way of faith.

'Bringing up children as Christians has its challenges. N *and* N will need to discover the story of Christ's birth, death and resurrection, the pattern of his loving life, and the teaching that he gave. We pray that they will come closer to God as they grow in faith, explore the Bible, and make their baptismal promises for themselves when they come to confirmation.

'As well as worshipping with the Church, Christians follow Jesus by standing up for truth and justice, and showing compassion to those in need. They are to be faithful and loving. The example that you give by prayer and the life that you lead will affect N *and* N for their whole life.

'Remember to ask for God's help, and pray for *them* often, as we now pray for you.'

This could lead into the prayer for parents (L5 below) and/or intercessions.

Commission – Option 2: infant candidates

Where the newly baptized are unable to answer for themselves, a minister addresses the congregation, parents and godparents.

The address includes

¶ *The welcome of the Church, local and universal*

¶ *The importance of belonging to the Christian community*

¶ *The responsibilities of parents and godparents*

¶ *The challenge to grow in Christian discipleship*   **L2**

Option 3: candidates able to answer for themselves

The question and answer form of commission at item L3 can be used either in the default position for the Commission (following the material for infants if there is a mixture of candidates), or it can be delayed and used at the end of the service, as the first part of the Sending Out.

Using it as part of the Sending Out can work particularly well if the candidates return to the font and the congregation turn to face it too, or if they gather by the main doors of the church (if the font is elsewhere), as a sign of taking our baptismal calling into the world.

Commission – Option 3: candidates able to answer for themselves

Here or at the beginning of the Sending Out, a minister may say to the newly baptized who are able to answer for themselves

Those who are baptized are called to worship and serve God.

Will you continue in the apostles' teaching and fellowship,
in the breaking of bread, and in the prayers?
With the help of God, I will.

Will you persevere in resisting evil,
and, whenever you fall into sin, repent and return to the Lord?
With the help of God, I will.

Will you proclaim by word and example
the good news of God in Christ?
With the help of God, I will.

Will you seek and serve Christ in all people,
loving your neighbour as yourself?
With the help of God, I will.

Will you acknowledge Christ's authority over human society,
by prayer for the world and its leaders,
by defending the weak, and by seeking peace and justice?
With the help of God, I will.

May Christ dwell in your heart(s) through faith,
that you may be rooted and grounded in love
and bring forth the fruit of the Spirit.
Amen.   **L**3

Option 4: candidates able to answer for themselves

In place of the forms of Commission provided in *Common Worship*, alternatives are provided in the Additional Baptism Texts in Accessible Language.

That material makes clear that the minister (or other suitable person) should talk directly and simply in his or her own words to the newly baptized, covering the topics listed in the bullet points.

Some ministers may find it helpful to speak from these bullet points, but it is important to make the words flow and not to give the impression that a written text is simply being read out.

An example might go like this:

> 'N, we are glad to have welcomed you to *(name of church)* for your baptism. There will always be a place for you here. Your baptism joins you to Christ and to his whole Church, in every part of the world, in the past and in the future, on earth and in heaven.
>
> 'Even before today, God began his work in you, but it will take the whole of your life to complete that work. There will be moments when the journey ahead is a delight and there will be times when it is hard, but you will never be alone. You will always have the support of other Christians. There will be many milestones on your journey: confirmation will be one of them.
>
> 'Remember that in Jesus, heaven has touched our world. Belonging to him will change your life and, through reading the Bible, you will learn more deeply the story of God's love. Through worship, prayer and caring for others you will grow more and more like Jesus. Stand up for fairness, truth and kindness.
>
> 'God's love is for you, and for everyone. Share with other people the good news of his love.'

Commission – Option 4: candidates able to answer for themselves

Where the newly baptized are able to answer for themselves,
a minister addresses them. The address includes

¶ *The welcome of the Church, local and universal*

¶ *The importance of belonging to the Christian community*

¶ *The challenge to grow in Christian discipleship*

¶ *The call to share God's love*   **L4**

Commission – Optional extra material

Items L5, L6 and L7 are all optional extras. They were originally provided in *Common Worship* to follow the Commission for infant candidates, but L6 and L7 might be appropriate for use, or adaptation, with candidates who can answer for themselves, or where there is a mixture of candidates.

Prayer for parents

This prayer for the parents or other primary carers could be used instead as part of the prayers of intercession – whether they follow on immediately or come later in the service.

Prayer for all the baptized

This is a prayer for all of us to be faithful to our baptism, and is not specific to the candidates or their parents and godparents.

Commission – Optional extra material

Prayer for parents

Faithful and loving God,
bless those who care for *these children*
and grant them your gifts of love, wisdom and faith.
Pour upon them your healing and reconciling love,
and protect their home from all evil.
Fill them with the light of your presence
and establish them in the joy of your kingdom,
through Jesus Christ our Lord.
Amen.   L5

Prayer for all the baptized

God of grace and life,
in your love you have given us
a place among your people;
keep us faithful to our baptism,
and prepare us for that glorious day
when the whole creation will be made perfect
in your Son our Saviour Jesus Christ.
Amen.   L6

Address to the Newly Baptized

This is a statement addressed to the candidates. Though it was designed for use with a child old enough to understand, it could be used or adapted for all candidates, as it provides a good summary of both the grace and the call which are inherent in baptism.

It ends rather abruptly and needs some further words to link it either with the prayers of intercession which follow, or with the Welcome (if the intercessions are placed after the Welcome).

If the Commission itself is included within the sermon, this address to the newly baptized works well as part of a flow in the service which goes like this:

- Baptism
- Prayer for Grace and Renewal by the Spirit ('May God, who has received you by baptism into his Church...') (K4)
- Address to the Newly Baptized (L7)
- Informal link: 'And so we gladly welcome you.'
- Welcome and Peace ('There is one Lord, one faith, one baptism....') (N1)

Address to the Newly Baptized

N and N,
today God has touched you with his love
and given you a place among his people.
God promises to be with you
in joy and in sorrow, to be your guide in life,
and to bring you safely to heaven.
In baptism God invites you on a life-long journey.
Together with all God's people
you must explore the way of Jesus
and grow in friendship with God, in love for his people,
and in serving others.
With us you will listen to the word of God
and receive the gifts of God.   **L7**

M Prayers of Intercession

Prayers of Intercession should normally be part of a baptism service, because they signal that the newly baptized are being drawn into a Church that is called to pray for the world. It might be appropriate for the newly baptized (or their parents, godparents, or older siblings) to introduce sections of these prayers, or to lead the congregation in the response by giving the 'cue' line each time.

The forms provided here are not compulsory – other forms, or more informal patterns of prayer could be used instead.

The intercessions have been placed here to follow the pattern for Baptism within a service of Holy Communion, but if there is no Holy Communion, they might more naturally follow after the Welcome and Peace.

The intercessions might conclude with a collect. This is not the Collect of the Day, but a short summing-up prayer.

Intercessions in a service without Holy Communion

If the service does not include Holy Communion, the prayer provided as a Post Communion prayer (Resource Section P) could instead be used as a conclusion for the intercessions.

The intercessions are then followed by the Lord's Prayer, which could be introduced with a sentence such as this:

> As your children, born again in Christ, we say
> **Our Father …**   **M**1a

(For the full text of the Lord's Prayer, see back page.)

Prayers of Intercession – general

Intercessions may be led by the president or others. These or other suitable words may be used. The intercession may conclude with a Collect and/or with the Lord's Prayer.

As a royal priesthood, let us pray to the Father
through Christ who ever lives to intercede for us.

Reveal your kingdom among the nations;
may peace abound and justice flourish.
Especially for …

Your name be hallowed.
Your kingdom come.

Send down upon us the gift of the Spirit
and renew your Church with power from on high.
Especially for …

Your name be hallowed.
Your kingdom come.

Deliver the oppressed, strengthen the weak,
heal and restore your creation.
Especially for …

Your name be hallowed.
Your kingdom come.

Rejoicing in the fellowship of the Church on earth,
we join our prayers with all the saints in glory.

Your name be hallowed.
Your kingdom come. **M1**

Prayers of Intercession – alternative

We thank you that you have claimed for yourself
those who have been washed in the waters of rebirth.
Uphold them in this new life,
that they may ever remain steadfast in faith,
joyful in hope, and rooted in your love.

Father of life,
make known your glory.

Pour your blessing on all your people.
May our hearts ever praise you,
and find their perfect rest in you.
Grant us the freedom of your service
and peace in doing your will.

Father of life,
make known your glory.

The whole creation is filled with the light of your grace.
Dispel the darkness of our hearts,
and forgive our sins and negligences,
that we may come at last to the light of your glory.

Father of life,
make known your glory.   M2

Intercessions in a service without Holy Communion

If the service does not include Holy Communion, the seasonal Prayer after Communion (item P2) could be used instead as a conclusion for these intercessions.

The intercessions are then followed by the Lord's Prayer, which could be introduced with a seasonal sentence such as this:

> In baptism God declares
>   that we are his children, whom he loves;
> so let us pray
> **Our Father ...**   M3*a*

(For the full text of the Lord's Prayer, see back page.)

Prayers of Intercession – Epiphany/Baptism of Christ/Trinity

God of glory,
whose radiance shines from the face of Christ,
give your children such assurance of your mercy
and such knowledge of your grace,
that, believing all you promise, and receiving all you give,
they may be transformed ever more closely by your Spirit
into the image of Jesus, your Son.

Father of life,
make known your glory.

God of light,
whose life shines beyond all things,
give us and all your Church the will to follow Christ
and to bear his peace,
that the light of Christ may bring confidence to the world,
and faithfulness to all who look to you in hope.

Father of life,
make known your glory.

God of power,
whose word gives life to heaven and earth,
pour your abundant gifts on all your creation,
that the blind may see, the fallen may be raised,
and your people find tongues to confess
your promises of a broken world made new.

Father of life,
make known your glory.   M3

Intercessions in a service without Holy Communion

If the service does not include Holy Communion, the seasonal Prayer after Communion (item P3) could instead be used as a conclusion for these intercessions.

The intercessions are then followed by the Lord's Prayer, which could be introduced with a seasonal sentence such as this:

> Raised again with Christ in the power of the Spirit, we say
>
> **Our Father ...**   M4*a*

(For the full text of the Lord's Prayer, see back page.)

Prayers of Intercession – Easter/Pentecost

Father, we thank you that by baptism
you have raised these your children with Christ
to new life in the Spirit.
Guide and protect them with your grace,
that they may follow you all their days
and grow in knowledge and love of you.

Father, by the victory of your Son,
give light to the world.

May Christ who conquered sin and death
keep his whole Church faithful to his gospel.
Help us always to hold fast to truth
and to walk in the way of life.

Father, by the victory of your Son,
give light to the world.

May the Holy Spirit fill the hearts and minds of all nations
to unite the world in peace and love.
By your healing power restore all that is broken
and unite us with you, our God and Father.

Father, by the victory of your Son,
give light to the world.   **M**4

Intercessions in a service without Holy Communion

If the service does not include Holy Communion, the seasonal Prayer after Communion (item P4) could instead be used as a conclusion for these intercessions.

The intercessions are then followed by the Lord's Prayer, which could be introduced with a seasonal sentence such as this:

> Remember us Lord in your heavenly kingdom
> as we your children unite our prayers with your Son
> **Our Father ...**   M5*a*

(For the full text of the Lord's Prayer, see back page.)

Prayers of Intercession – All Saints'/Advent

Heavenly Father,
receive into the arms of your mercy
all who have been baptized
and make them your own for ever;
that, having tasted of your goodness,
they may ever hunger for your continuing presence
in their walk of faith.

Your kingdom come.
Your will be done.

Stir up within your Church
the zeal that inspires your saints in every generation.
Give us a due sense of your grace,
and the strength to do your will.
You measure us by our needs;
may we never measure you by our impatience.

Your kingdom come.
Your will be done.

Surrounded by so great a company of witnesses,
may we honour your blessings
in all the ages that have gone before,
and live in joyful expectation
of your promises in the ages yet to come.

Your kingdom come.
Your will be done.   M5

N The Welcome and Peace

If baptism takes place within a service of Holy Communion, the Welcome and Peace normally comes after the Prayers of Intercession, preparing for the transition into the Liturgy of the Eucharist.

If there is no Holy Communion, the Welcome and the sharing of the Peace can instead follow the baptism itself (and the Commission, if this is being used as a section in its own right), and comes before the Prayers of Intercession.

The Welcome is the moment to encourage the congregation to greet the newly baptized with applause (if this has not already happened immediately after the baptism itself). If the congregation have been seated for the Prayers of Intercession or the Commission, make sure you get them to stand for the Welcome.

Following the Welcome with the Peace allows for congregation members to greet and congratulate the newly baptized and their families more personally and informally.

The Welcome and Peace

The Welcome

There is one Lord, one faith, one baptism:
N and N, by one Spirit we are all baptized into one body.
We welcome you into the fellowship of faith;
we are children of the same heavenly Father;
we welcome you.

The congregation may greet the newly baptized.   **N**1

The Peace

The president introduces the Peace in these or other suitable words.

(For seasonal Introductions to the Peace, see items N4–N8.)

We are all one in Christ Jesus.
We belong to him through faith,
heirs of the promise of the Spirit of peace.   **N**2

The peace of the Lord be always with you
and also with you.

A minister may say

Let us offer one another a sign of peace.

All may exchange a sign of peace.   **N**3

Seasonal Introductions to the Peace

These seasonal Introductions to the Peace could be appropriate in any act of worship, but they also pick up baptismal themes such as new life, the gift of the Holy Spirit, and our belonging within the household of God.

Seasonal Introductions to the Peace

Introduction to the Peace – Epiphany/Baptism of Christ/Trinity

If anyone is in Christ, there is a new creation.
The old has passed away; the new has come.   **N4**

Introduction to the Peace – Easter

The risen Christ came and stood among his disciples
    and said 'Peace be with you'.
Then were they glad when they saw the Lord.   **N5**

Introduction to the Peace – Pentecost

God has made us one in Christ.
He has set his seal upon us,
and as a pledge of what is to come
has given us the Spirit to dwell in our hearts.   **N6**

Introduction to the Peace – All Saints'/Advent

May the God of peace make you perfect and holy,
that you may be kept safe and blameless in spirit, soul, and body,
for the coming of our Lord Jesus Christ.   **N7**

(or)

We are fellow-citizens with the saints
and of the household of God
through Christ our Lord,
who came and preached peace to those who were far off
and those who were near.   **N8**

O Prefaces for the Eucharistic Prayer

Short Prefaces

The prefaces on this page are suitable for use with any of the Eucharistic Prayers that allow for short proper prefaces for special days, seasons, or themes (Prayers A, B, or C, or the Prayer of Consecration from the BCP). Other appropriate preface material could be used.

If you are using one of the prayers specially provided for use when lots of children are present – *Additional Eucharistic Prayers* (Church House Publishing, 2012) – Prayer Two lends itself to the use of a simple short preface that picks up on baptismal themes. This could be adapted from one of those on this page, or locally written.

Short Preface 1 (items O1 and O2)

This short proper preface (in both contemporary and traditional language) is provided in the *Common Worship* baptism service itself.

Short Preface 2 (item O3)

This preface (tagged with the theme 'Christian beginnings' in *New Patterns for Worship,* page 263) would be suitable with Prayers A, B or C. It might also be used (in this, or an adapted form) with Prayer Two from the *Additional Eucharistic Prayers.*

Short Prefaces for the Eucharistic Prayer

Short Preface 1

This short Proper Preface may be used (contemporary language)

And now we give you thanks
because by water and the Holy Spirit
you have made us a holy people in Jesus Christ our Lord;
you raise us to new life in him
and renew in us the image of your glory.   O1

This short Proper Preface may be used (traditional language)

And now we give thee thanks
because by water and the Holy Spirit
thou hast made us a holy people in Jesus Christ our Lord,
thou dost raise us to new life in him
and renew in us the image of thy glory.   O2

Short Preface 2

And now we give you thanks
because through him we are saved for ever
and baptized into your service.   O3

Extended Prefaces (items O4 and O5)

For Eucharistic Prayers A, B and E, extended preface material might pick up even more deeply the baptismal themes. *New Patterns for Worship* (Church House Publishing, 2002) Section G is one possible source for such extended prefaces. The two reproduced here and on the next page (items O4 and O5) are adapted from thanksgivings tagged with the theme 'Christian beginnings' in *New Patterns for Worship*, pages 254–5. There is further guidance on using them as preface material on page 222 in the same volume.

The extended prefaces provided here are neither compulsory nor restrictive. Other suitable material could be adapted from these, or composed locally.

Extended Preface 1 demonstrates a responsorial approach; Extended Preface 2 gives an example of a presidential text.

Extended Prefaces for the Eucharistic Prayer

Extended Preface 1

Father, for your gift of water in creation
we give you thanks and praise.

For your Spirit, sweeping over the waters,
bringing light and life
we give you thanks and praise.

For your Son, Jesus Christ our Lord,
baptized in the river Jordan
we give you thanks and praise.

For your new creation,
brought to birth by water and the Spirit
we give you thanks and praise.

For your grace bestowed upon us your children,
washing away our sins
we give you thanks and praise.

*With Eucharistic Prayers A and B the preface concludes and leads into
the Sanctus like this:*

Therefore with angels and archangels …

*With Eucharistic Prayer E the preface concludes and leads into the Sanctus
like this:*

And so we gladly thank you, with saints and angels …   **O4**

Extended Preface 2

Blessed are you,
God and Father of our Lord Jesus Christ.
By your great mercy we have been born anew
      to a living hope
through the resurrection of your Son from the dead,
and to an inheritance which is imperishable, undefiled,
       and unfading.
Once we were no people, but now we are your people,
declaring your wonderful deeds in Christ,
who called us out of darkness into his marvellous light.

By the baptism of his death and resurrection
you gave birth to your Church,
delivered us from slavery to sin and death,
and made with us a new covenant.
At his ascension
you exalted him to sit at your right hand,
where according to his promise he is with us always,
baptizing us with the Holy Spirit and with fire.

The joy of resurrection fills the whole world,
and therefore we join with angels and archangels
and the whole company of heaven,
in the song of unending praise, *saying*:
Holy, holy, holy Lord,
God of power and might,
heaven and earth are full of your glory.
Hosanna in the highest.
[Blessed is he who comes in the name of the Lord.
Hosanna in the highest.]   O5

P   Prayer after Communion

In a baptism service that does not include Holy Communion, any of these Post Communion prayers could instead be used as concluding prayers at the end of the Prayers of Intercession.

Prayer after Communion

The authorized Post Communion of the Day, or a seasonal form,
or the following is used

Eternal God, our beginning and our end,
preserve in your people the new life of baptism;
as Christ receives us on earth,
so may he guide us through the trials of this world
and enfold us in the joy of heaven,
where you live and reign,
one God for ever and ever.
Amen.   **P**/

Prayer after Communion – Epiphany/Baptism of Christ/Trinity

God of glory,
you inspire us with the breath of life
which brought to birth a new world in Christ.
May we who are reborn in him
be transformed by the renewal of our lives,
that the light of your new creation
may flood the world with your abundant grace;
through Christ our Lord.
Amen.   **P**2

Prayer after Communion – Easter/Pentecost

Author of life divine,
in the resurrection of your Son,
you set before us the mystery of his triumph over sin and death;
may all who are washed in the waters of rebirth
rise to newness of life
and find the promised presence of your abundant grace;
through Jesus Christ our Lord.
Amen.   **P**3

Prayer after Communion – All Saints'/Advent

Lord, in the vision of your heavenly kingdom
you reveal among us the promise of your glory;
may that glory be ours
as we claim our citizenship in the kingdom
where you are alive and reign, one God, for ever and ever.
Amen.   **P**4

Q The Sending Out

There are four possible parts to the Sending Out:

- Words of Commission for use with those able to answer for themselves (item L3, page 107) *(optional)*
- A blessing *(optional)*
- The Giving of a Lighted Candle *(optional – and has an alternative position earlier in the service)*
- The Dismissal

Words of Commission

Where someone has been baptized who can answer for themselves, the inclusion of a form of Commission at this point in the service reinforces the ongoing nature of Christian discipleship and its missional focus.

The Blessing

It often surprises people that the Blessing is optional, and in most situations a blessing will be a natural part of the end of the service. However, the option to omit it is a further reminder that the key aspect of this part of the service is not God's blessing for us, but the taking of the light of Christ into the world.

This is emphasised most clearly if the Giving of a Lighted Candle takes place here, but there is also the option to do that immediately after the baptism itself.

For seasonal forms of blessing, see items Q2 to Q7 (pages 141–145).

The Sending Out

If the words of item L3 (page 107) have not been used earlier, a minister may address the newly baptized who are able to answer for themselves, using those words.

The Blessing

The president may use a seasonal blessing (see below), or another suitable blessing, or

The God of all grace,
who called you to his eternal glory in Christ Jesus,
establish, strengthen and settle you in the faith;
and the blessing of God almighty,
the Father, the Son, and the Holy Spirit,
be among you and remain with you always.
Amen.   **Q**1

Seasonal blessings

Some of these seasonal blessings are drawn from the *Common Worship* baptism material; others are blessings which are tagged with the theme 'Christian beginnings' in *New Patterns for Worship* (Church House Publishing, 2002) Section J. Other appropriate seasonal blessings may be found in *Common Worship: Times and Seasons*.

Seasonal blessings

The Blessing – Epiphany/Baptism of Christ/Trinity

God, who in his Christ gives us a spring of water
welling up to eternal life,
perfect in you the image of his glory;
and the blessing of God almighty,
the Father, the Son, and the Holy Spirit,
be among you and remain with you always.
Amen.   **Q**2

May God the Father,
who led the wise men by the shining of a star
to find the Christ, the Light from Light,
lead you also in your pilgrimage to find the Lord.
Amen.

May God the Son,
who turned water into wine at the wedding feast at Cana,
transform your lives and make glad your hearts.
Amen.

May God the Holy Spirit,
who came upon the beloved Son
at his baptism in the river Jordan,
pour out his gifts on you
who have come to the waters of new birth.
Amen.

And the blessing …   **Q**3

The Blessing – Easter/Pentecost

God the Father,
by whose glory Christ was raised from the dead,
strengthen you by his life-giving Spirit
to walk with him in the paths of righteousness and peace;
and the blessing of God almighty,
the Father, the Son, and the Holy Spirit,
be among you and remain with you always.
Amen.   **Q4**

God poured out his promised Holy Spirit in tongues of flame
on the day of Pentecost.
Amen.

You have been baptized with the Spirit and with fire.
Amen.

May that same Holy Spirit send you out to tell his story,
and give you a voice to glorify God before all people.
Amen.

And the blessing …

cf Acts 2.1-4
Q5

The Father, whose glory fills the heavens,
cleanse you by his holiness and send you to proclaim his word.
Amen.

The Son, who has ascended to the heights,
pour upon you the riches of his grace.
Amen.

The Holy Spirit, the Comforter,
equip you and strengthen you in your ministry.
Amen.

And the blessing …   **Q6**

The Blessing – All Saints'/Advent

May God,
who kindled the fire of his love in the hearts of the saints,
give you joy in their fellowship,
and strengthen you to follow them in the way of holiness;
and the blessing of God almighty,
the Father, the Son, and the Holy Spirit,
be among you and remain with you always.
Amen.   **Q**7

R Giving of a Lighted Candle

Common Worship places the Giving of a Lighted Candle, by default, at the conclusion of the service, where it acts as a symbol of mission – the light of Christ being taken by the newly baptized, with the whole Church, to the world. The text refers to the renunciation of darkness, making a possible link back to the lighting of a candle at the Decision (if this has happened).

The candle can be lit from the Easter candle (in churches which use one), and will sometimes be a miniature copy of the Easter candle. Make sure you explain that the candle is for the family to take home. They could be encouraged to light it on birthdays, on the anniversary of baptism or on other special occasions.

Alternative position

The alternative option is for the candle to be given immediately following the baptism itself – see Section K for more information.

Giving of a Lighted Candle

The president or another person may give each of the newly baptized a lighted candle.

These may be lit from the candle used at the Decision.

When all the newly baptized have received a candle, the president says

God has delivered us from the dominion of darkness
and has given us a place with the saints in light.

You have received the light of Christ;
walk in this light all the days of your life.
**Shine as a light in the world
to the glory of God the Father.**   **R**/

S The Dismissal

In this form, the dismissal is clearly designed to pick up the imagery of the lighted candle. If the lighted candle has been given earlier in the service, immediately after the administration of baptism, it is worth thinking about how to return to its imagery in order to emphasise that the light is for sharing not just for keeping.

Perhaps the candle could be re-lit (without further words) immediately before the dismissal, or the baptismal party could gather at the Easter candle for the dismissal.

For baptisms as part of A Service of the Word, other forms of dismissal might be appropriate.

The Dismissal

Go in the light and peace of Christ
Thanks be to God.   **S** 1

From Easter Day to Pentecost Alleluia, alleluia *may be added to both
the versicle and the response.*

T Other texts

Canticles in Procession to the Font

A Song of Trust in God

Refrain:

My soul longs for you, O God.

1   As the deer longs for the water brooks, ◆
    so longs my soul for you, O God.

2   My soul is athirst for God, even for the living God; ◆
    when shall I come before the presence of God?

3   My tears have been my bread day and night, ◆
    while all day long they say to me, 'Where is now your God?'

4   Now when I think on these things, I pour out my soul: ◆
    how I went with the multitude
        and led the procession to the house of God.

5   With the voice of praise and thanksgiving, ◆
    among those who kept holy day.

6   Why are you so full of heaviness, O my soul, ◆
    and why are you so disquieted within me?

7   O put your trust in God; ◆
    for I will yet give him thanks,
        who is the help of my countenance, and my God.

Psalm 42.1-7

Glory to the Father and to the Son
and to the Holy Spirit;
as it was in the beginning is now
and shall be for ever. Amen.

My soul longs for you, O God.   **T1**

A Song of Deliverance

Refrain:

All the earth, shout and sing for joy,
for great in your midst is the Holy One.

1 'Behold, God is my salvation; ♦
    I will trust and not be afraid;

2 'For the Lord God is my strength and my song, ♦
    and has become my salvation.'

3 With joy you will draw water ♦
    from the wells of salvation.

4 On that day you will say, ♦
    'Give thanks to the Lord, call upon his name;

5 'Make known his deeds among the nations, ♦
    proclaim that his name is exalted.

6 'Sing God's praises, who has triumphed gloriously; ♦
    let this be known in all the world.

7 'Shout and sing for joy, you that dwell in Zion, ♦
    for great in your midst is the Holy One of Israel.'

Isaiah 12.2-6

Glory to the Father and to the Son
and to the Holy Spirit;
as it was in the beginning is now
and shall be for ever. Amen.

All the earth, shout and sing for joy,
for great in your midst is the Holy One.   **T**2

A Song of the New Creation

Refrain:

**I will make a way in the wilderness,
and rivers in the desert.**

1   'I am the Lord, your Holy One, ♦
     the Creator of Israel, your King.'

2   Thus says the Lord, who makes a way in the sea, ♦
     a path in the mighty waters,

3   'Remember not the former things, ♦
     nor consider the things of old.

4   'Behold, I am doing a new thing; ♦
     now it springs forth, do you not perceive it?

5   'I will make a way in the wilderness and rivers in the desert, ♦
     to give drink to my chosen people,

6   'The people whom I formed for myself, ♦
     that they might declare my praise.'

Isaiah 43.15,16,18,19,20c,21

**Glory to the Father and to the Son
and to the Holy Spirit;
as it was in the beginning is now
and shall be for ever. Amen.**

**I will make a way in the wilderness,
and rivers in the desert.**   **T3**

A Litany of the Resurrection

which may be used in Procession to the Baptismal Font

O give thanks to the Lord, for he is gracious:
and his mercy endures for ever.

He has loved us from all eternity:
for his mercy endures for ever.

And remembered us when we were in trouble:
for his mercy endures for ever.

For us and for our salvation he came down from heaven:
for his mercy endures for ever.

He became incarnate of the Holy Spirit and the Virgin Mary
and was made man:
for his mercy endures for ever.

By his cross and passion he has redeemed the world:
for his mercy endures for ever.

And has washed us from our sins in his own blood:
for his mercy endures for ever.

On the third day he rose again:
for his mercy endures for ever.

And has given us the victory:
for his mercy endures for ever.

He ascended into heaven:
for his mercy endures for ever.

And opened wide for us the everlasting doors:
for his mercy endures for ever.

He is seated at the right hand of the Father:
for his mercy endures for ever.

And ever lives to make intercession for us:
for his mercy endures for ever.

**Glory to the Father and to the Son
and to the Holy Spirit;
as it was in the beginning is now
and shall be for ever.
Amen.**   T4

For the gift of his Spirit:
blessed be Christ.

For the catholic Church:
blessed be Christ.

For the means of grace:
blessed be Christ.

For the hope of glory:
blessed be Christ.

For the triumphs of his gospel:
blessed be Christ.

For the lives of his saints:
blessed be Christ.

In joy and in sorrow:
blessed be Christ.

In life and in death:
blessed be Christ.

Now and to the end of the ages:
blessed be Christ.   **T**5

*This litany may be used in two parts (items T4 and T5), reserving the clauses
following the Gloria (T5) for a return procession from the place of baptism.*

Thanksgiving for the Holy Ones of God

which may be used in Procession to the Baptismal Font

The following responses may be said or sung

Let us bless the Lord.
Thanks be to God.

(or)

Alleluia, alleluia, alleluia.

For Abraham and Sarah, our ancestors in faith,
and all who journey into the unknown trusting God's promises:

For Jacob, deceitful younger brother, yet chosen by God,
the father of all who are called by virtue not of their own:

For Moses the lawgiver and Aaron the priest,
and all who lead God's people to freedom and newness of life:
Response

For Esther and Deborah, saviours of their nation,
and for all who dare to act courageously at God's call:

For Hannah and Ruth, and all who through love and devotion
witness to the faithfulness of God:

For Isaiah, John the Baptist and all the prophets,
and all who speak the truth without counting the cost:
Response

For Mary the Virgin, the mother of our Lord and God,
and all who obey God's call without question:

For Andrew and John and the first disciples,
and for all who forsake everything to follow Jesus:

For Mary Magdalene, Salome and Mary,
first witnesses of the resurrection,
and for all who bear witness to Christ:
Response

For Peter and Paul [, N] and the apostles,
who preached the gospel to Jew and Gentile,
and for all who take the good news to the ends of the earth:

For Barnabas, Silas and Timothy,
and for all who bring encouragement and steadfastness:

In the following sections names may be added or omitted to reflect local traditions.

For the writers of the Gospels
and for all who bring the faith of Christ alive for each generation:
Response

For Ambrose, Augustine, Gregory and Jerome,
and for all who contend for the truth of the gospel:

For Basil, Gregory of Nazianzus, Athanasius and John Chrysostom,
and all who enable us to reflect on the mystery of Christ:

For Cyprian, Antony and Ephrem,
and for all who lead the Church into new paths of discipleship:
Response

For Stephen, Alban, Agnes, Lucy and the whole army of martyrs,
and all who have faced death for love of Christ:

For Augustine of Canterbury and Aidan, for Boniface and Patrick,
and for all who have carried the gospel to this and other lands:

For Aelred, Bernard and Cuthbert,
and for all who live and teach the love of God:
Response

For Anselm and Richard Hooker,
and for all who reveal to us the depths of God's wisdom:

For Benedict and Francis, Hilda and Bede,
and for all who deepen our common life in Christ:

For Julian of Norwich, Bridget of Sweden and Teresa of Avila,
and for all who renew our vision of the mystery of God:
Response

For Thomas Cranmer
and all who reform the Church of God:

For Thomas More
and all who hold firm to its continuing faith:

For Gregory and Dunstan, George Herbert and John Keble,
and for all who praise God in poetry and song:

Response

For Lancelot Andrewes, John Wesley and Charles Simeon,
and for all who preach the word of God:

For William Wilberforce and Josephine Butler,
and for all who work to transform the world:

For Monica, and for Mary Sumner,
and for all who nurture faith in home and family:

Response

For the martyrs and peacemakers of our own time,
who shine as lights in the darkness:

For all the unsung heroes and heroines of our faith,
whose names are known to God alone:

For all those in our own lives
who have revealed to us the love of God
and shown to us the way of holiness:

Response

For *NN*...

Response

Let us rejoice and praise them with thankful hearts
and glorify our God in whom they put their trust.   T6

Emergency Baptism

The following form is sufficient.

The minister pours water on the person to be baptized, saying

N, I baptize you in the name of the Father, and of the Son,
and of the Holy Spirit.
Amen.

The minister may then say the Lord's Prayer and the Grace or a blessing.

If it is appropriate, some of the following may also be used.

Before the Baptism

Jesus says: I have come that you may have life
and have it in all its fullness. *John 10.10*

All that the Father gives me will come to me;
and whoever comes to me I will not turn away. *John 6.37*

The Lord is near to the brokenhearted
and will save those who are crushed in spirit. *Psalm 34.18*

Heavenly Father,
grant that by your Holy Spirit
this child may be born again
and know your love in the new creation
given us in Jesus Christ our Lord.
Amen.

At the Signing with the Cross

N, may Christ protect and defend you.
Receive the sign of his cross.

Prayer over the Water

Heavenly Father,
bless this water,
that whoever is washed in it
may be made one with Christ
in the fellowship of your Church,
and be brought through every tribulation
to share the risen life
that is ours in Jesus Christ our Lord.
Amen.

After the Baptism

As our Saviour taught us, so we pray

Our Father in heaven,
hallowed be your name,
your kingdom come,
your will be done,
on earth as in heaven.
Give us today our daily bread.
Forgive us our sins
as we forgive those who sin against us.
Lead us not into temptation
but deliver us from evil.
For the kingdom, the power,
and the glory are yours
now and for ever.
Amen.

(or)

Let us pray with confidence as our Saviour has taught us

Our Father, who art in heaven,
hallowed be thy name;
thy kingdom come;
thy will be done;
on earth as it is in heaven.
Give us this day our daily bread.
And forgive us our trespasses,
as we forgive those who trespass against us.
And lead us not into temptation;
but deliver us from evil.
For thine is the kingdom,
the power and the glory,
for ever and ever.
Amen.

Eternal God, our beginning and our end,
preserve in your people the new life of baptism;
as Christ receives us on earth,
so may he guide us through the trials of this world,
and enfold us in the joy of heaven,
where you live and reign,
one God for ever and ever.
Amen.

The grace of our Lord Jesus Christ,
and the love of God,
and the fellowship of the Holy Spirit
be with us all evermore.
Amen.

(or)

May God almighty,
the Father, the Son, and the Holy Spirit,
bless and keep you this day and for evermore.
Amen.

Notes to Emergency Baptism

1   In an emergency, a lay person may be the minister of baptism, and should subsequently inform those who have the pastoral responsibility for the person so baptized.

2   Parents are responsible for requesting emergency baptism for an infant. They should be assured that questions of ultimate salvation or of the provision of a Christian funeral for an infant who dies do not depend upon whether or not the child has been baptized.

3   Before baptizing, the minister should ask the name of the person to be baptized. When, through the absence of parents or for some other reason, there is uncertainty as to the name of the person, the baptism can be properly administered without a name (so long as the identity of the person baptized can be duly recorded).

Service in Church

4   If the person lives, they shall afterwards come to church, or be brought to church, and the service for Holy Baptism followed, except that the Signing with the Cross, the Prayer over the Water and the Baptism are omitted.

5   It may be appropriate to use the Thanksgiving Prayer for a Child (item B2, page 35).

6   At the Presentation the president says

> We welcome N, who has been baptized and now comes
> to take *his/her* place in the company of God's people.

7   Oil mixed with fragrant spices (traditionally called chrism), expressing the blessings of the messianic era and the richness of the Holy Spirit, may be used to accompany the prayer after the baptism. It is appropriate that the oil should have been consecrated by the bishop.

Notes to Holy Baptism

Holy Baptism is normally administered by the parish priest in the course of public worship on Sunday 'when the most number of people come together' (Canon B 21).

1 Minister of Baptism

Where rubrics speak of 'the president', this indicates the parish priest or other minister authorized to administer Holy Baptism. When the bishop is present he or she normally presides over the whole service. Parts of the service not assigned to the president may be delegated to others.

2 Ordering of the Service

Pages 16–19 show how baptism is to be administered within a celebration of Holy Communion. Pages 22–25 show how it is to be administered at A Service of the Word and at Morning or Evening Prayer. When baptism is administered within a celebration of Holy Communion, the Notes to the Order for the Celebration of Holy Communion apply equally to this service. The structure of the service, however, enables it to be used as a significant celebration on its own and there may be occasions where such a celebration of Holy Baptism forms a main Sunday act of worship. Whenever Holy Baptism is administered there shall be a sermon.

3 Thanksgiving Prayer for a Child

This option (see item B2, page 35) may be used where it is appropriate to express thanksgiving for a child to be baptized later in the service; this may be inserted as part of the Preparation. This is not intended to preclude the use of a separate service of Thanksgiving for the Gift of a Child.

4 Presentation of the Candidates

The Presentation may follow the Introduction where circumstances make this appropriate.

5 Collect, Readings and Other Variable Texts

The Collect and readings for the Sunday should normally be used, especially on Sundays between the First Sunday of Advent and the Feast of the Presentation of Christ, and between the First Sunday of Lent and Trinity Sunday. The Collects provided in the rite and its Supplementary Texts may, however, be substituted on Sundays between the Presentation of Christ and the beginning of Lent and between Trinity Sunday and the beginning of Advent even when the normal Sunday readings are used. The Collects and readings provided in the service or in its Supplementary Texts are for use on occasions when baptism is the predominant element in the service. The basic form of the service remains constant. Within this structure seasonal material may also be used. This is linked to occasions in the Christian year when its use might be particularly appropriate.

6 Godparents and Sponsors

The term 'godparent' is used for those asked to present children for baptism and to continue to support them. The term 'sponsor' is used for those who agree to support in the journey of faith candidates (of any age) for baptism, confirmation or affirmation of baptismal faith. It is not necessary that a candidate have the same person as godparent and sponsor. When children who are old enough to speak are baptized, such children, at the discretion of the parish priest, also answer the questions at the Decision with parents and godparents.

7 Hymns and Silence

If occasion requires, hymns may be sung and silence may be kept at points other than those which are indicated.

8 Corporate Responses

When members of a family are baptized at the same time, the questions at the Decision may be answered in the form 'We reject ... '.

9 Profession of Faith

The whole congregation joins in the Apostles' Creed at the Profession of Faith or makes the responses in the Alternative Profession of Faith (item J2, page 93).

10 Use of Oil

Where it has been agreed that oil will be used, pure olive oil, reflecting the practice of athletes preparing for a contest, may be used for the Signing with the Cross. Oil mixed with fragrant spices (traditionally called chrism), expressing the blessings of the messianic era and the richness of the Holy Spirit, may be used to accompany the prayer after the baptism. It is appropriate that the oil should have been consecrated by the bishop.

11 Signing with the Cross

At the Signing with the Cross, after the president or other minister has made the sign using the words provided, parents, godparents and sponsors may also be invited to make the sign of the cross. It is sufficient if the people join in and say their part once only, when all the candidates have been signed. The possibility of signing with the cross at the prayer after the baptism is provided for, but if this is done it should be accompanied by the text provided at that point in the rite, not the text provided for the Signing with the Cross after the Decision. If signing takes place after the baptism, it must follow the administration of water as a separate action.

12 Administration of Water

A threefold administration of water (whether by dipping or pouring) is a very ancient practice of the Church and is commended as testifying to the faith of the Trinity in which candidates are baptized. Nevertheless, a single administration is also lawful and valid. The use of a substantial amount of water is desirable; water must at least flow on the skin of the candidate. The president may delegate the act of baptism to another lawful minister.

13 Conditional Baptism

If it is not certain whether a person has already been baptized with water in the name of the Father, and of the Son, and of the Holy Spirit, then the usual service of baptism is used, but the form of words at the baptism shall be

> N, if you have not already been baptized, I baptize you in the name of the Father, and of the Son, and of the Holy Spirit.

All **Amen.**

14 Clothing

Provision is made for clothing after the baptism. This may be a practical necessity where dipping is the mode of baptism employed; the text provided draws on ancient tradition, linking practical necessity and scriptural imagery.

15 Commission

The text provided should normally be used; however, it may be paraphrased by the minister if pastoral circumstances require. Alternatively its contents may be included in the sermon. If the newly baptized are able to answer for themselves, the Commission may be deferred until the beginning of the Sending Out.

16 Prayers of Intercession

General intercession should normally be part of the service. Such prayers draw the newly baptized into the praying Church of which they are now a part. It may be appropriate for the newly baptized to introduce sections of these prayers. Prayers in responsive form are provided; one of the forms of prayer on pages 115–123 may be used. The Prayers may be used after the Welcome and Peace.

17 Giving of a Lighted Candle

The Paschal candle or another large candle is made ready so that it may be lit at the Decision. Individual candles may be lit from it and given to candidates as part of the Sending Out. The giving of lighted candles may take place at an earlier stage in the service, after the administration of baptism.

18 Renewal of Baptismal Vows

When the Renewal of Baptismal Vows takes place within a service of
Holy Baptism and/or Confirmation, the responses of the people may
follow the responses of the candidates, for example:

> Do you reject … ?
>
> *Candidates*   **I reject …**
>
> *All*   **I reject …**

or the people may make the responses with the candidates.

SAMPLE SERVICES SECTION

Sample Services Section

Introduction to the Sample Services Section

Different sorts of material

This section of the book is divided into three parts.

Generic sample services

The first part contains a series of generic sample services that could be reproduced locally, with suitable adaptations. In these the rubrics are generalized and tend to follow those in the *Common Worship* services themselves. In most of these services (with the exception of Sample 5), where there are options, the order follows the default *Common Worship* structure (for instance, with the Giving of a Lighted Candle at the end of the service).

Samples 1 to 5 all assume infant candidates. Samples 1 and 3 use the Additional Baptism Texts in Accessible Language, and are designed to work alongside the published service cards.

Sample 5 has been included to demonstrate the flow of a service when some of the alternative options are used for structuring the service.

Samples 6 and 7 show how the choices look when the candidates are all able to answer for themselves, using first the standard texts from *Common Worship* (Sample 6) and then the Additional Baptism Texts in Accessible Language (Sample 7).

In each of these samples, general, rather than seasonal, options have been selected.

Guidance notes for particular circumstances

These give general advice on good practice for a range of particular situations, including some guidance on making baptism as accessible as possible to everyone, including people with disabilities.

Specific scenarios

The final part of this section provides a number of scenarios. In these we have imagined a range of different local church contexts and particular candidates for baptism. These are, therefore, meant to be illustrative rather than prescriptive, designed to help local churches to think about how to use the *Common Worship* material well in their own context.

In these services the rubrics have been made specific to the context, and are used to give explanation or commentary on the service as well as instructions for the leaders. These services, therefore, are *not* designed to be reproduced locally in this particular form. In each case the imagined context is outlined first (the type of church and its situation; the particular nature of the baptism service envisaged; the resources available). This is followed by some notes on the service itself and the reasons for the decisions made, and then by the full service.

How to use the material

All of the material in this section is primarily designed to show a variety of possibilities within the range of *Common Worship* material. If you are using material from this section, make sure you adjust it as appropriate for your own context. Even the generic samples are not necessarily suitable simply to take and use without making sure they fit your own situation and the specific context of the baptism in question. At the very least, you will want to remove the item codes from the different texts – these have been included here simply to make it easier to find alternatives and to see how the material from the Resources Section can be put together.

Sample Services

Sample 1 – Holy Baptism (using the Additional Baptism Texts in Accessible Language, compatible with the published service card)

This sample service is designed to illustrate the full text needed by the president for use alongside the published service card 'Holy Baptism'. For more guidance on using the published service cards, see the guidance notes below (pages 266–268). (For a service that includes Holy Communion, see Sample 3.)

The published card contains only the minimal material needed by the congregation, with simplified rubrics and headings. The simplified rubrics from the card have been reproduced here, placed in square brackets [...]. Sometimes these replace the standard *Common Worship* rubrics; sometimes both have been included (so that the president can guide the congregation to the appropriate section of the card, but is also aware of the full instructions). For the same reason, this sample service only includes the section and item headings included on the printed card, and includes them in the form in which they appear on the card (which is sometimes different from the standard *Common Worship* headings).

The items are presented in their default *Common Worship* positions. The published card and this sample service assume that the candidates are unable to answer for themselves, so the rubrics reflect this, and other options are not included. In this service, some other indications of alternatives or options have also been omitted for simplicity.

¶ Getting Ready

The president says

The grace of our Lord Jesus Christ,
the love of God
and the fellowship of the Holy Spirit be with you all
and also with you.   A1

[Everyone is welcomed and the service is introduced.]

The president may use these or other words

Our Lord Jesus Christ has told us
that to enter the kingdom of heaven
we must be born again of water and the Spirit,
and has given us baptism as the sign and seal of this new birth.
Here we are washed by the Holy Spirit and made clean.
Here we are clothed with Christ,
dying to sin that we may live his risen life.
As children of God,
we have a new dignity and God calls us to fullness of life.   C2

[A prayer is said, and everyone says Amen.]

Either the Collect of the Day, or this Collect is said

Heavenly Father,
by the power of your Holy Spirit
you give to your faithful people
new life in the water of baptism.
Guide and strengthen us by the same Spirit,
that we who are born again
may serve you in faith and love,
and grow into the full stature of your Son, Jesus Christ,
who is alive and reigns with you
in the unity of the Holy Spirit now and for ever.
Amen.   D1

¶ Listening

[One or more appropriate passages from the Bible are read, followed by a talk.]
The readings of the day are normally used on Sundays and Principal Festivals.

[At the end the reader may say]

This is the word of the Lord.
Thanks be to God.

¶ Baptizing

[Halfway down p. 1 of the card]

[Families and godparents may be invited to come to the front.]

The candidates may be presented to the congregation.
Where appropriate, they may be presented by their godparents or sponsors.

The president addresses the whole congregation

Jesus said, 'Let the children come to me. Do not stop them'.
We thank God for N *and* N who *have* come to be baptized today.
Christ loves *them* and welcomes *them* into his Church.
So I ask you all:

Will you support *these children* as *they begin their* journey of faith?
We will.

Will you help *them* to live and grow within God's family?
We will.

[The parents and godparents are asked important questions]

God knows each of us by name and we are his.
Parents and godparents, you speak for N *and* N today.
Will you pray for *them,* and help *them* to follow Christ?
We will.   F4

A large candle may be lit.

The president addresses the candidates through their parents, godparents
and sponsors

We all wander far from God and lose our way:
Christ comes to find us and welcomes us home.
In baptism we respond to his call.

Therefore I ask:

Do you turn away from sin?
I do.

Do you reject evil?
I do.

The candidates, together with their parents, godparents and sponsors, may turn at this point.

Do you turn to Christ as Saviour?
I do.

Do you trust in him as Lord?
I do.   G2

Signing with the Cross

[Halfway down p. 2 of the card]

[If not already at the front, parents and candidates come forward. Each candidate is signed with the cross, with these words]

The president or another minister makes the sign of the cross on the forehead of each candidate, saying

Christ claims you for his own.
Receive the sign of his cross.   H1

The president may invite parents, godparents and sponsors to sign the candidates with the cross.

When all the candidates have been signed, the president says

Do not be ashamed of Christ.
You are his for ever.
Stand bravely with him
against all the powers of evil,
and remain faithful to Christ to the end of your life.   H4

May almighty God deliver you from the powers of darkness,
and lead you in the light and obedience of Christ.
Amen.   H5

[Everyone may be invited to gather at the font.]

Prayer over the Water

[Top of p. 3 of the card]

[These words may be used]

Praise God who made heaven and earth,
who keeps his promise for ever.

Let us give thanks to the Lord our God.
It is right to give thanks and praise. 11

[One of these prayers is said over the water]

[Either]
Loving Father,
we thank you for your servant Moses,
who led your people through the waters of the Red Sea
to freedom in the Promised Land.
We thank you for your Son Jesus,
who has passed through the deep waters of death
and opened for all the way of salvation.
Now send your Spirit,
that those who are washed in this water
may die with Christ and rise with him,
to find true freedom as your children,
alive in Christ for ever.
Amen. 13

[Or]

We praise you, loving Father,
for the gift of your Son Jesus.
He was baptized in the River Jordan,
where your Spirit came upon him
and revealed him as the Son you love.
He sent his followers
to baptize all who turn to him.
Now, Father, we ask you to bless this water,
that those who are baptized in it
may be cleansed in the water of life,
and, filled with your Spirit,
may know that they are loved as your children,
safe in Christ for ever.
Amen. 14

Believing

[Top of p. 4 of the card]

[Everyone is asked to join in answering these questions]

Let us affirm,
together with *these who are* being baptized,
our common faith in Jesus Christ.

Do you believe and trust in God the Father,
source of all being and life,
the one for whom we exist?
I believe and trust in him.

Do you believe and trust in God the Son,
who took our human nature,
died for us and rose again?
I believe and trust in him.

Do you believe and trust in God the Holy Spirit,
who gives life to the people of God
and makes Christ known in the world?
I believe and trust in him.

This is the faith of the Church.
This is our faith.
We believe and trust in one God,
Father, Son and Holy Spirit.   J2

The Baptism

[Each candidate is baptized with water, with these words]

N, I baptize you in the name of the Father,
and of the Son,
and of the Holy Spirit.
Amen.   K2

May God, who has received you by baptism into his Church,
pour upon you the riches of his grace,
that within the company of Christ's pilgrim people
you may daily be renewed by his anointing Spirit,
and come to the inheritance of the saints in glory.
Amen.   K4

[Everyone may return to their seats.
A minister (or another person) speaks to the congregation, parents and
godparents and may lead one or more prayers.]

A minister addresses the congregation, parents and godparents (unless the
sermon has already included similar material).

The address includes
¶ *The welcome of the Church, local and universal*
¶ *The importance of belonging to the Christian community*
¶ *The responsibilities of parents and godparents*
¶ *The challenge to grow in Christian discipleship*

L2

The following prayer for parents may be added

Faithful and loving God,
bless those who care for these children
and grant them your gifts of love, wisdom and faith.
Pour upon them your healing and reconciling love,
and protect their home from all evil.
Fill them with the light of your presence
and establish them in the joy of your kingdom,
through Jesus Christ our Lord.
Amen. **L**5

The Welcome and Peace

[Halfway down p. 5 of the card]

There is one Lord, one faith, one baptism:
N and N, by one Spirit we are all baptized into one body.
We welcome you into the fellowship of faith;
we are children of the same heavenly Father;
we welcome you. **N**1

[Everyone may greet the newly baptized.]

The president introduces the Peace in these or other suitable words.
(For seasonal Introductions to the Peace, see items N4–N8.)

We are all one in Christ Jesus.
We belong to him through faith,
heirs of the promise of the Spirit of peace. **N**2

The peace of the Lord be always with you
and also with you.

A minister may say

Let us offer one another a sign of peace.

All may exchange a sign of peace.   **N**3

Praying for the World

[Near the bottom of p. 5 of the card]

[Either this response may be used

Your name be hallowed.
Your kingdom come.

Or this

Father of life,
make known your glory.]

The two alternative full forms of intercession are:

As a royal priesthood, let us pray to the Father
through Christ who ever lives to intercede for us.

Reveal your kingdom among the nations;
may peace abound and justice flourish.
Especially for ...

Your name be hallowed.
Your kingdom come.

Send down upon us the gift of the Spirit
and renew your Church with power from on high.
Especially for ...

Your name be hallowed.
Your kingdom come.

Deliver the oppressed, strengthen the weak,
heal and restore your creation.
Especially for ...

Your name be hallowed.
Your kingdom come.

Rejoicing in the fellowship of the Church on earth,
we join our prayers with all the saints in glory.

Your name be hallowed.
Your kingdom come.   **M1**

Or this:

We thank you that you have claimed for yourself
those who have been washed in the waters of rebirth.
Uphold them in this new life,
that they may ever remain steadfast in faith,
joyful in hope, and rooted in your love.

Father of life,
make known your glory.

Pour your blessing on all your people.
May our hearts ever praise you,
and find their perfect rest in you.
Grant us the freedom of your service
and peace in doing your will.

Father of life,
make known your glory.

The whole creation is filled with the light of your grace.
Dispel the darkness of our hearts,
and forgive our sins and negligences,
that we may come at last to the light of your glory.

Father of life,
make known your glory.   **M2**
Other forms could be used instead.

The Lord's Prayer

[Modern form at the top of p. 6 of the card;
traditional form halfway down p. 6]

As your children, born again in Christ, we say
Our Father ...   **M1a**

¶ Going Out

[Halfway down p. 7 of the card]

[A blessing may be said and then each of the newly baptized may be given a lighted candle.]

The president may use a seasonal blessing (see items Q2–Q7), or another suitable blessing, or

The God of all grace,
who called you to his eternal glory in Christ Jesus,
establish, strengthen and settle you in the faith;
and the blessing of God almighty,
the Father, the Son, and the Holy Spirit,
be among you and remain with you always.
Amen. Q1

When all the newly baptized have received a candle, the president says

God has delivered us from the dominion of darkness
and has given us a place with the saints in light.

You have received the light of Christ;
walk in this light all the days of your life.
**Shine as a light in the world
to the glory of God the Father.** R1

Go in the light and peace of Christ.
Thanks be to God. S1

Sample 2 – Holy Baptism (using the standard *Common Worship* texts)

This sample service is designed to illustrate the full text needed by the president for a service that uses the standard *Common Worship* texts and the default options for the structure of the service.

This service assumes that the candidates are unable to answer for themselves, so the rubrics reflect this, and other options are not included. Some other indications of alternatives or options have also been omitted for simplicity. To see all possible options, see the Resource Section of this volume.

¶ Preparation

At the entry of the ministers a hymn may be sung.

The Greeting

The president says

The grace of our Lord Jesus Christ, the love of God
and the fellowship of the Holy Spirit be with you all
and also with you. A1

Further words of welcome or introduction may be said.

Introduction to Baptism

The president may use these or other words

Our Lord Jesus Christ has told us
that to enter the kingdom of heaven
we must be born again of water and the Spirit,
and has given us baptism as the sign and seal of this new birth.
Here we are washed by the Holy Spirit and made clean.
Here we are clothed with Christ,
dying to sin that we may live his risen life.
As children of God,
we have a new dignity and God calls us to fullness of life. C2

The Collect

The president introduces a period of silent prayer with the words 'Let us pray' or a more specific bidding.

Either the Collect of the Day, or this Collect is said

Heavenly Father,
by the power of your Holy Spirit
you give to your faithful people
new life in the water of baptism.
Guide and strengthen us by the same Spirit,
that we who are born again
may serve you in faith and love,
and grow into the full stature of your Son, Jesus Christ,
who is alive and reigns with you
in the unity of the Holy Spirit now and for ever.
Amen.   **D1**

¶ The Liturgy of the Word

Readings

The readings of the day are normally used on Sundays and Principal Festivals.

Either one or two readings from Scripture may precede the Gospel reading.

At the end of each the reader may say

This is the word of the Lord.
Thanks be to God. E1

Gospel Reading

When the Gospel is announced the reader says

Hear the Gospel of our Lord Jesus Christ according to N.
Glory to you, O Lord.

At the end

This is the Gospel of the Lord.
Praise to you, O Christ. E2

Sermon

¶ The Liturgy of Baptism

Presentation of the Candidates

The candidates may be presented to the congregation. Where appropriate, they
may be presented by their godparents or sponsors.

The president addresses the whole congregation

Faith is the gift of God to his people.
In baptism the Lord is adding to our number
   those whom he is calling.
People of God,
will you welcome these *children*
and uphold *them* in *their* new life in Christ?
With the help of God, we will.   F2

The president then says to the parents and godparents

Parents and godparents, the Church receives these *children* with joy.
Today we are trusting God for *their* growth in faith.
Will you pray for *them*, draw *them* by your example into the community of faith
and walk with *them* in the way of Christ?
With the help of God, we will.

In baptism *these children* begin *their* journey in faith.
You speak for *them* today.
Will you care for *them*, and help *them* to take *their* place
within the life and worship of Christ's Church?
With the help of God, we will.   F3

The Decision

A large candle may be lit.

The president addresses the candidates through their parents, godparents
and sponsors

In baptism, God calls us out of darkness into his marvellous light.
To follow Christ means dying to sin and rising to new life with him.

Therefore I ask:

Do you reject the devil and all rebellion against God?
I reject them.

Do you renounce the deceit and corruption of evil?
I renounce them.

Do you repent of the sins that separate us from God and neighbour?
I repent of them.

Do you turn to Christ as Saviour?
I turn to Christ.

Do you submit to Christ as Lord?
I submit to Christ.

Do you come to Christ, the way, the truth and the life?
I come to Christ.   G1

Signing with the Cross

The president or another minister makes the sign of the cross on the forehead of each candidate, saying

Christ claims you for his own.
Receive the sign of his cross.   H1

The president may invite parents, godparents and sponsors to sign the candidates with the cross.

When all the candidates have been signed, the president says

Do not be ashamed to confess the faith of Christ crucified.
Fight valiantly as a disciple of Christ
against sin, the world and the devil,
and remain faithful to Christ to the end of your life.   H2

May almighty God deliver you from the powers of darkness,
restore in you the image of his glory,
and lead you in the light and obedience of Christ.
Amen.   H3

Prayer over the Water

The ministers and candidates gather at the baptismal font.

The president stands before the water of baptism and says (optional seasonal and responsive forms are provided – items 15–19)

Praise God who made heaven and earth,
who keeps his promise for ever.

Let us give thanks to the Lord our God.
It is right to give thanks and praise.   11

We thank you, almighty God, for the gift of water
to sustain, refresh and cleanse all life.
Over water the Holy Spirit moved in the beginning of creation.
Through water you led the children of Israel
from slavery in Egypt to freedom in the Promised Land.
In water your Son Jesus received the baptism of John
and was anointed by the Holy Spirit as the Messiah, the Christ,
to lead us from the death of sin to newness of life.

We thank you, Father, for the water of baptism.
In it we are buried with Christ in his death.
By it we share in his resurrection.
Through it we are reborn by the Holy Spirit.
Therefore, in joyful obedience to your Son,
we baptize into his fellowship those who come to him in faith.

Now sanctify this water that, by the power of your Holy Spirit,
they may be cleansed from sin and born again.
Renewed in your image, may they walk by the light of faith
and continue for ever in the risen life of Jesus Christ our Lord;
to whom with you and the Holy Spirit
be all honour and glory, now and for ever.
Amen.

12

Profession of Faith

The president addresses the congregation

Brothers and sisters, I ask you to profess
together with *these candidates*
the faith of the Church.

Do you believe and trust in God the Father?
**I believe in God, the Father almighty,
creator of heaven and earth.**

Do you believe and trust in his Son Jesus Christ?
**I believe in Jesus Christ, his only Son, our Lord,
who was conceived by the Holy Spirit,
born of the Virgin Mary, suffered under Pontius Pilate,
was crucified, died, and was buried;
he descended to the dead.
On the third day he rose again;
he ascended into heaven,
he is seated at the right hand of the Father,
and he will come to judge the living and the dead.**

Do you believe and trust in the Holy Spirit?
**I believe in the Holy Spirit,
the holy catholic Church,
the communion of saints,
the forgiveness of sins,
the resurrection of the body,
and the life everlasting.
Amen.** J/

Baptism

The president or another minister dips each candidate in water, or pours water on them, saying

N, I baptize you in the name of the Father,
and of the Son,
and of the Holy Spirit.
Amen.   K2

The president says

May God, who has received you by baptism into his Church,
pour upon you the riches of his grace,
that within the company of Christ's pilgrim people
you may daily be renewed by his anointing Spirit,
and come to the inheritance of the saints in glory.
Amen.   K4

Commission

A minister addresses the congregation, parents and godparents, using these or similar words (unless the sermon has already included similar material)

We have brought *these children* to baptism knowing that Jesus died and rose again for *them* and trusting in the promise that God hears and answers prayer. We have prayed that in Jesus Christ *they* will know the forgiveness of *their* sins and the new life of the Spirit.

As *they grow* up, *they* will need the help and encouragement of the Christian community, so that *they* may learn to know God in public worship and private prayer, follow Jesus Christ in the life of faith, serve *their* neighbour after the example of Christ, and in due course come to confirmation.

As part of the Church of Christ, we all have a duty to support *them* by prayer, example and teaching. As *their* parents and godparents, you have the prime responsibility for guiding and helping *them* in *their* early years. This is a demanding task for which you will need the help and grace of God.

[Therefore let us now pray for grace in guiding *these children* in the way of faith.]
                                                                      L1

The following prayer for parents may be said

Faithful and loving God,
bless those who care for *these children*
and grant them your gifts of love, wisdom and faith.
Pour upon them your healing and reconciling love,
and protect their home from all evil.
Fill them with the light of your presence
and establish them in the joy of your kingdom,
through Jesus Christ our Lord.
Amen.   L5

The Welcome

There is one Lord, one faith, one baptism:
N and N, by one Spirit we are all baptized into one body.
We welcome you into the fellowship of faith;
we are children of the same heavenly Father;
we welcome you.   N1

The congregation may greet the newly baptized.

The Peace

The president introduces the Peace in these or other suitable words.
(For seasonal Introductions to the Peace, see items N4–N8.)

We are all one in Christ Jesus.
We belong to him through faith,
heirs of the promise of the Spirit of peace.   N2

The peace of the Lord be always with you
and also with you.

A minister may say
Let us offer one another a sign of peace.

All may exchange a sign of peace.   N3

Prayers of Intercession

Intercessions may be led by the president or others.
These or other suitable words may be used

As a royal priesthood, let us pray to the Father
through Christ who ever lives to intercede for us.

Reveal your kingdom among the nations;
may peace abound and justice flourish.
Especially for …

Your name be hallowed.
Your kingdom come.

Send down upon us the gift of the Spirit
and renew your Church with power from on high.
Especially for …

Your name be hallowed.
Your kingdom come.

Deliver the oppressed, strengthen the weak,
heal and restore your creation.
Especially for …

Your name be hallowed.
Your kingdom come.

Rejoicing in the fellowship of the Church on earth,
we join our prayers with all the saints in glory.

Your name be hallowed.
Your kingdom come.   **M***1*

The Lord's Prayer

As your children, born again in Christ, we say
Our Father …   **M***1a*

(For the full text of the Lord's Prayer, see back page.)

¶ The Sending Out

The Blessing

The president may use a seasonal blessing (see items Q2–Q7),
or another suitable blessing, or

The God of all grace,
who called you to his eternal glory in Christ Jesus,
establish, strengthen and settle you in the faith;
and the blessing of God almighty,
the Father, the Son, and the Holy Spirit,
be among you and remain with you always.
Amen.   Q1

Giving of a Lighted Candle

The president or another person may give each of the newly baptized
a lighted candle.
These may be lit from the candle used at the Decision.

When all the newly baptized have received a candle, the president says

God has delivered us from the dominion of darkness
and has given us a place with the saints in light.

You have received the light of Christ;
walk in this light all the days of your life.
Shine as a light in the world
to the glory of God the Father.   R1

The Dismissal

Go in the light and peace of Christ.
Thanks be to God.   S1

Sample 3 – Holy Baptism with Holy Communion (using the Additional Baptism Texts in Accessible Language, compatible with the published service card)

This sample service is designed to illustrate the text needed by the president for a service that can be used alongside the published service card 'Holy Baptism in a Service of Holy Communion'. Those cards incorporate the Additional Baptism Texts in Accessible Language, and use the alternative form of Profession of Faith. Full texts for the eucharistic part of the service have not been included, but headings indicate the material needed. For more guidance on using the published service cards, see the guidance notes below (pages 266–268).

The published card contains only the material needed for the Liturgy of Baptism, and parts of The Sending Out, with simplified rubrics and headings. In those sections, the simplified rubrics from the published card have been reproduced here, placed in square brackets *[…]*. Sometimes these replace the standard *Common Worship* rubrics, sometimes both have been included (so that the president can guide the congregation to the appropriate section of the card, but is also aware of the full instructions). For the same reason, this sample service indicates when *Common Worship* section headings are *not* included on the printed card, and conforms section headings that are included to the form in which they appear on the card (which is sometimes different from the standard *Common Worship* headings).

The items are presented in their default *Common Worship* positions. The published card and this sample service assume that the candidates are unable to answer for themselves, so the rubrics reflect this, and other options are not included. In this service, some other indications of alternatives or options have also been omitted for simplicity.

¶ Preparation

The Greeting

The president says

The grace of our Lord Jesus Christ,
the love of God
and the fellowship of the Holy Spirit be with you all
and also with you.   **A**/

Further words of welcome or introduction may be said.

Introduction to Baptism

The president may use these or other words

Our Lord Jesus Christ has told us
that to enter the kingdom of heaven
we must be born again of water and the Spirit,
and has given us baptism as the sign and seal of this new birth.
Here we are washed by the Holy Spirit and made clean.
Here we are clothed with Christ,
dying to sin that we may live his risen life.
As children of God,
we have a new dignity and God calls us to fullness of life.   **C**2

The Gloria in excelsis may be used.

The Collect

The president introduces a period of silent prayer with the words 'Let us pray'
or a more specific bidding.

Either the Collect of the Day, or this Collect is said

Heavenly Father,
by the power of your Holy Spirit
you give to your faithful people
new life in the water of baptism.
Guide and strengthen us by the same Spirit,
that we who are born again
may serve you in faith and love,
and grow into the full stature of your Son, Jesus Christ,
who is alive and reigns with you
in the unity of the Holy Spirit now and for ever.
Amen.   **D1**

¶ The Liturgy of the Word

Readings

The readings of the day are normally used on Sundays and Principal Festivals.

At the end of each the reader may say

This is the word of the Lord.
Thanks be to God.   E1

Gospel Reading

When the Gospel is announced the reader says

Hear the Gospel of our Lord Jesus Christ according to N.
Glory to you, O Lord.

At the end

This is the Gospel of the Lord.
Praise to you, O Christ.   E2

Sermon

¶ The Liturgy of Baptism

(The published card starts here, at the top of p. 1. The heading on the card says, 'The Baptism'.)

Presentation of the Candidates

(this heading is not on the card)

[Families and godparents may be invited to come to the front.]

The candidates may be presented to the congregation. Where appropriate, they may be presented by their godparents or sponsors.

The president addresses the whole congregation

Jesus said, 'Let the children come to me. Do not stop them'.
We thank God for *N and N* who *have* come to be baptized today.
Christ loves *them* and welcomes *them* into his Church.
So I ask you all:

Will you support *these children* as *they begin their* journey of faith?
We will.

Will you help *them* to live and grow within God's family?
We will.

[The parents and godparents are asked important questions]

God knows each of us by name and we are his.
Parents and godparents, you speak for *N and N* today.
Will you pray for *them*, and help *them* to follow Christ?
We will.   **F4**

The Decision

(this heading is not on the card)

A large candle may be lit.

The president addresses the candidates through their parents, godparents and sponsors

We all wander far from God and lose our way:
Christ comes to find us and welcomes us home.
In baptism we respond to his call.

Therefore I ask:

Do you turn away from sin?
I do.

Do you reject evil?
I do.

The candidates, together with their parents, godparents and sponsors, may turn at this point.

Do you turn to Christ as Saviour?
I do.

Do you trust in him as Lord?
I do.   **G**2

Signing with the Cross

(Top of p. 2 of the card)

[If not already at the front, parents and candidates come forward. Each candidate is signed with the cross, with these words]

The president or another minister makes the sign of the cross on the forehead of each candidate, saying

Christ claims you for his own.
Receive the sign of his cross.   **H**1

The president may invite parents, godparents and sponsors to sign the candidates with the cross.

When all the candidates have been signed, the president says

Do not be ashamed of Christ.
You are his for ever.
**Stand bravely with him
against all the powers of evil,
and remain faithful to Christ to the end of your life.**   H4

May almighty God deliver you from the powers of darkness,
and lead you in the light and obedience of Christ.
Amen.   H5
[Everyone may be invited to gather at the font.]

Prayer over the Water

[Halfway down p. 2 of the card]

[These words may be used]

Praise God who made heaven and earth,
who keeps his promise for ever.

Let us give thanks to the Lord our God.
It is right to give thanks and praise.
                I1

[One of these prayers is said over the water]

[Either]

Loving Father,
we thank you for your servant Moses,
who led your people through the waters of the Red Sea
to freedom in the Promised Land.
We thank you for your Son Jesus,
who has passed through the deep waters of death
and opened for all the way of salvation.
Now send your Spirit,
that those who are washed in this water
may die with Christ and rise with him,
to find true freedom as your children,
alive in Christ for ever.
Amen.   13

[Or – on p. 3 of the card]

We praise you, loving Father,
for the gift of your Son Jesus.
He was baptized in the River Jordan,
where your Spirit came upon him
and revealed him as the Son you love.
He sent his followers
to baptize all who turn to him.
Now, Father, we ask you to bless this water,
that those who are baptized in it
may be cleansed in the water of life,
and, filled with your Spirit,
may know that they are loved as your children,
safe in Christ for ever.
Amen.   14

Declaring our Faith

(Near the bottom of p. 3 of the card)

[Everyone is asked to join in answering these questions]

Let us affirm,
together with *these who are* being baptized,
our common faith in Jesus Christ.

Do you believe and trust in God the Father,
source of all being and life,
the one for whom we exist?
I believe and trust in him.

Do you believe and trust in God the Son,
who took our human nature,
died for us and rose again?
I believe and trust in him.

Do you believe and trust in God the Holy Spirit,
who gives life to the people of God
and makes Christ known in the world?
I believe and trust in him.

This is the faith of the Church.
This is our faith.
We believe and trust in one God,
Father, Son and Holy Spirit.   J2

The Baptism

[Each candidate is baptized with water, with these words]

N, I baptize you in the name of the Father,
and of the Son,
and of the Holy Spirit.
Amen.   K2

The president says

May God, who has received you by baptism into his Church,
pour upon you the riches of his grace,
that within the company of Christ's pilgrim people
you may daily be renewed by his anointing Spirit,
and come to the inheritance of the saints in glory.
Amen.   K4

Commission

[Everyone may return to their seats.
A minister (or another person) speaks to the congregation, parents and
godparents and may lead one or more prayers.]

A minister addresses the congregation, parents and godparents (unless the
sermon has already included similar material).

The address includes
¶ *The welcome of the Church, local and universal*
¶ *The importance of belonging to the Christian community*
¶ *The responsibilities of parents and godparents*
¶ *The challenge to grow in Christian discipleship*   L2

The following prayer for parents may be added

Faithful and loving God,
bless those who care for *these children*
and grant them your gifts of love, wisdom and faith.
Pour upon them your healing and reconciling love,
and protect their home from all evil.
Fill them with the light of your presence
and establish them in the joy of your kingdom,
through Jesus Christ our Lord.
Amen.   L5

Praying for the World

(Near the bottom of p. 4 of the card)

[Either this response may be used

Your name be hallowed.
Your kingdom come.

Or this

Father of life,
make known your glory.]

The two alternative full forms of intercession are:

As a royal priesthood, let us pray to the Father
through Christ who ever lives to intercede for us.

Reveal your kingdom among the nations;
may peace abound and justice flourish.
Especially for …

Your name be hallowed.
Your kingdom come.

Send down upon us the gift of the Spirit
and renew your Church with power from on high.
Especially for …

Your name be hallowed.
Your kingdom come.

Deliver the oppressed, strengthen the weak,
heal and restore your creation.
Especially for …

Your name be hallowed.
Your kingdom come.

Rejoicing in the fellowship of the Church on earth,
we join our prayers with all the saints in glory.

Your name be hallowed.
Your kingdom come.   **M I**

Or this:

We thank you that you have claimed for yourself
those who have been washed in the waters of rebirth.
Uphold them in this new life,
that they may ever remain steadfast in faith,
joyful in hope, and rooted in your love.

Father of life,
make known your glory.

Pour your blessing on all your people.
May our hearts ever praise you,
and find their perfect rest in you.
Grant us the freedom of your service
and peace in doing your will.

Father of life,
make known your glory.

The whole creation is filled with the light of your grace.
Dispel the darkness of our hearts,
and forgive our sins and negligences,
that we may come at last to the light of your glory.

Father of life,
make known your glory.   **M**2

Other forms could be used instead.

The Welcome and Peace

(Top of p. 5 of the card)

There is one Lord, one faith, one baptism:
N and N, by one Spirit we are all baptized into one body.
We welcome you into the fellowship of faith;
we are children of the same heavenly Father;
we welcome you.   **N**1

[Everyone may greet the newly baptized.]

The president introduces the Peace in these or other suitable words.

(For seasonal Introductions to the Peace, see items N4–N8.)

We are all one in Christ Jesus.
We belong to him through faith,
heirs of the promise of the Spirit of peace.   **N**2

The peace of the Lord be always with you
and also with you.

A minister may say

Let us offer one another a sign of peace.

All may exchange a sign of peace.   **N**3

*[After everyone has shared a sign of peace, the service will continue in a
different service booklet.]*

¶ The Liturgy of the Eucharist

The Order for Celebration of Holy Communion continues with

Preparation of the Table

Taking of the Bread and Wine

The Eucharistic Prayer

This short Proper Preface may be used

And now we give you thanks
because by water and the Holy Spirit
you have made us a holy people in Jesus Christ our Lord;
you raise us to new life in him
and renew in us the image of your glory.   **O** *1*

The Lord's Prayer

This introduction may be used

As your children, born again in Christ, we say
Our Father ...   **M** *1 a*

(For the full text of the Lord's Prayer, see back page.)

Breaking of the Bread

Giving of Communion

Prayer after Communion

The authorized Post Communion of the Day, or a seasonal form,
or the following is used

Eternal God, our beginning and our end,
preserve in your people the new life of baptism;
as Christ receives us on earth,
so may he guide us through the trials of this world
and enfold us in the joy of heaven,
where you live and reign,
one God for ever and ever.
Amen.   **P** *1*

[After Communion a hymn may be sung before the final blessing.]

¶ We Go Out into the World

(Near the bottom of p. 5 of the card, underneath the photograph)

[A blessing may be said and then each of the newly baptized may be given a lighted candle.]

The president may use a seasonal blessing (see items Q2–Q7), or another suitable blessing, or

The God of all grace,
who called you to his eternal glory in Christ Jesus,
establish, strengthen and settle you in the faith;
and the blessing of God almighty,
the Father, the Son, and the Holy Spirit,
be among you and remain with you always.
Amen. Q*I*

The president or another person may give each of the newly baptized a lighted candle.

These may be lit from the candle used at the Decision.

When all the newly baptized have received a candle, the president says

God has delivered us from the dominion of darkness
and has given us a place with the saints in light.

You have received the light of Christ;
walk in this light all the days of your life.
**Shine as a light in the world
to the glory of God the Father.** R*I*

The Dismissal

Go in the light and peace of Christ.
Thanks be to God. S*I*

Sample 4 – Holy Baptism with Holy Communion (using the standard *Common Worship* texts)

This sample service is designed to illustrate the text needed by the president for a service of Baptism (including Holy Communion) that uses the standard *Common Worship* texts and the default options for the structure of the service. Full texts for the eucharistic part of the service have not been included.

This service assumes that the candidates are unable to answer for themselves, so the rubrics reflect this, and other options are not included. Some other indications of alternatives or options have also been omitted for simplicity. To see all possible options, see the Resource Section of this volume.

¶ Preparation

At the entry of the ministers a hymn may be sung.

The Greeting

The president says

The grace of our Lord Jesus Christ,
the love of God
and the fellowship of the Holy Spirit be with you all
and also with you.   **A**1

Further words of welcome or introduction may be said.

Introduction to Baptism

The president may use these or other words

Our Lord Jesus Christ has told us
that to enter the kingdom of heaven
we must be born again of water and the Spirit,
and has given us baptism as the sign and seal of this new birth.
Here we are washed by the Holy Spirit and made clean.
Here we are clothed with Christ,
dying to sin that we may live his risen life.
As children of God,
we have a new dignity and God calls us to fullness of life.   **C**2

The Gloria in excelsis may be used.

The Collect

*The president introduces a period of silent prayer with the words 'Let us pray'
or a more specific bidding.*

Either the Collect of the Day, or this Collect is said

Heavenly Father,
by the power of your Holy Spirit
you give to your faithful people
new life in the water of baptism.
Guide and strengthen us by the same Spirit,
that we who are born again
may serve you in faith and love,
and grow into the full stature of your Son, Jesus Christ,
who is alive and reigns with you
in the unity of the Holy Spirit now and for ever.
Amen.   **D**/

¶ The Liturgy of the Word

Readings

The readings of the day are normally used on Sundays and Principal Festivals.

Either one or two readings from Scripture may precede the Gospel reading.

At the end of each the reader may say

This is the word of the Lord.
Thanks be to God.   E1

Gospel Reading

When the Gospel is announced the reader says

Hear the Gospel of our Lord Jesus Christ according to N.
Glory to you, O Lord.

At the end

This is the Gospel of the Lord.
Praise to you, O Christ.   E2

Sermon

¶ The Liturgy of Baptism

Presentation of the Candidates

The candidates may be presented to the congregation. Where appropriate, they may be presented by their godparents or sponsors.

The president addresses the whole congregation

Faith is the gift of God to his people.
In baptism the Lord is adding to our number
   those whom he is calling.
People of God,
will you welcome *these children*
and uphold *them* in *their* new life in Christ?
With the help of God, we will.   F2

The president then says to the parents and godparents

Parents and godparents, the Church receives these *children* with joy.
Today we are trusting God for *their* growth in faith.
Will you pray for *them*, draw *them* by your example into the community of faith
and walk with *them* in the way of Christ?
With the help of God, we will.

In baptism *these children* begin *their* journey in faith.
You speak for *them* today.
Will you care for *them*, and help *them* to take *their* place
within the life and worship of Christ's Church?
With the help of God, we will.   F3

The Decision

A large candle may be lit.

The president addresses the candidates through their parents, godparents and sponsors

In baptism, God calls us out of darkness into his marvellous light.
To follow Christ means dying to sin and rising to new life with him.

Therefore I ask:

Do you reject the devil and all rebellion against God?
I reject them.

Do you renounce the deceit and corruption of evil?
I renounce them.

Do you repent of the sins that separate us from God and neighbour?
I repent of them.

Do you turn to Christ as Saviour?
I turn to Christ.

Do you submit to Christ as Lord?
I submit to Christ.

Do you come to Christ, the way, the truth and the life?
I come to Christ.   G1

Signing with the Cross

The president or another minister makes the sign of the cross on the forehead of each candidate, saying

Christ claims you for his own.
Receive the sign of his cross.   H1

The president may invite parents, godparents and sponsors to sign the candidates with the cross.

When all the candidates have been signed, the president says

Do not be ashamed to confess the faith of Christ crucified.
Fight valiantly as a disciple of Christ
against sin, the world and the devil,
and remain faithful to Christ to the end of your life.   H2

May almighty God deliver you from the powers of darkness,
restore in you the image of his glory,
and lead you in the light and obedience of Christ.
Amen.   H*3*

Prayer over the Water

The ministers and candidates gather at the baptismal font.

*The president stands before the water of baptism and says (optional seasonal
and responsive forms are provided – items 15–19)*

Praise God who made heaven and earth,
who keeps his promise for ever.

Let us give thanks to the Lord our God.
It is right to give thanks and praise.   *11*

We thank you, almighty God, for the gift of water
to sustain, refresh and cleanse all life.
Over water the Holy Spirit moved in the beginning of creation.
Through water you led the children of Israel
from slavery in Egypt to freedom in the Promised Land.
In water your Son Jesus received the baptism of John
and was anointed by the Holy Spirit as the Messiah, the Christ,
to lead us from the death of sin to newness of life.

We thank you, Father, for the water of baptism.
In it we are buried with Christ in his death.
By it we share in his resurrection.
Through it we are reborn by the Holy Spirit.
Therefore, in joyful obedience to your Son,
we baptize into his fellowship those who come to him in faith.

Now sanctify this water that, by the power of your Holy Spirit,
they may be cleansed from sin and born again.
Renewed in your image, may they walk by the light of faith
and continue for ever in the risen life of Jesus Christ our Lord;
to whom with you and the Holy Spirit
be all honour and glory, now and for ever.
Amen.   *12*

Profession of Faith

The president addresses the congregation

Brothers and sisters, I ask you to profess
together with *these* candidates
the faith of the Church.

Do you believe and trust in God the Father?
I believe in God, the Father almighty,
creator of heaven and earth.

Do you believe and trust in his Son Jesus Christ?
I believe in Jesus Christ, his only Son, our Lord,
who was conceived by the Holy Spirit,
born of the Virgin Mary, suffered under Pontius Pilate,
was crucified, died, and was buried;
he descended to the dead.
On the third day he rose again;
he ascended into heaven,
he is seated at the right hand of the Father,
and he will come to judge the living and the dead.

Do you believe and trust in the Holy Spirit?
I believe in the Holy Spirit,
the holy catholic Church,
the communion of saints,
the forgiveness of sins,
the resurrection of the body,
and the life everlasting.
Amen. J*1*

Baptism

The president or another minister dips each candidate in water, or pours water
on them, saying

N, I baptize you in the name of the Father,
and of the Son,
and of the Holy Spirit.
Amen. K2

The president says

May God, who has received you by baptism into his Church,
pour upon you the riches of his grace,
that within the company of Christ's pilgrim people
you may daily be renewed by his anointing Spirit,
and come to the inheritance of the saints in glory.
Amen.   K4

Commission

A minister addresses the congregation, parents and godparents, using these or similar words (unless the sermon has already included similar material)

We have brought *these children* to baptism knowing that Jesus died and rose again for *them* and trusting in the promise that God hears and answers prayer. We have prayed that in Jesus Christ *they* will know the forgiveness of *their* sins and the new life of the Spirit.

As *they grow* up, *they* will need the help and encouragement of the Christian community, so that *they* may learn to know God in public worship and private prayer, follow Jesus Christ in the life of faith, serve *their* neighbour after the example of Christ, and in due course come to confirmation.

As part of the Church of Christ, we all have a duty to support *them* by prayer, example and teaching. As *their* parents and godparents, you have the prime responsibility for guiding and helping *them* in *their* early years. This is a demanding task for which you will need the help and grace of God.

[Therefore let us now pray for grace in guiding *these children* in the way of faith.]

                                                                              L1

The following prayer for parents may conclude the Commission

Faithful and loving God,
bless those who care for *these children*
and grant them your gifts of love, wisdom and faith.
Pour upon them your healing and reconciling love,
and protect their home from all evil.
Fill them with the light of your presence
and establish them in the joy of your kingdom,
through Jesus Christ our Lord.
Amen.   L5

Prayers of Intercession

Intercessions may be led by the president or others.

These or other suitable words may be used

As a royal priesthood, let us pray to the Father
through Christ who ever lives to intercede for us.

Reveal your kingdom among the nations;
may peace abound and justice flourish.
Especially for …

Your name be hallowed.
Your kingdom come.

Send down upon us the gift of the Spirit
and renew your Church with power from on high.
Especially for …

Your name be hallowed.
Your kingdom come.

Deliver the oppressed, strengthen the weak,
heal and restore your creation.
Especially for …

Your name be hallowed.
Your kingdom come.

Rejoicing in the fellowship of the Church on earth,
we join our prayers with all the saints in glory.

Your name be hallowed.
Your kingdom come.   **M***l*

The Welcome

There is one Lord, one faith, one baptism:
N and N, by one Spirit we are all baptized into one body.
We welcome you into the fellowship of faith;
we are children of the same heavenly Father;
we welcome you.   **N***l*

The congregation may greet the newly baptized.

The Peace

The president introduces the Peace in these or other suitable words.
(For seasonal Introductions to the Peace, see items N4–N8.)

We are all one in Christ Jesus.
We belong to him through faith,
heirs of the promise of the Spirit of peace.   **N2**

The peace of the Lord be always with you
and also with you.

A minister may say

Let us offer one another a sign of peace.

All may exchange a sign of peace.   **N3**

¶ The Liturgy of the Eucharist

The Order for Celebration of Holy Communion continues with

Preparation of the Table

Taking of the Bread and Wine

The Eucharistic Prayer

This short Proper Preface may be used

And now we give you thanks
because by water and the Holy Spirit
you have made us a holy people in Jesus Christ our Lord;
you raise us to new life in him
and renew in us the image of your glory.   **O1**

The Lord's Prayer

This introduction may be used

As your children, born again in Christ, we say
Our Father …   **M1*a***

(For the full text of the Lord's Prayer, see back page.)

Breaking of the Bread

Giving of Communion

Prayer after Communion

The authorized Post Communion of the Day, or a seasonal form,
or the following is used

Eternal God, our beginning and our end,
preserve in your people the new life of baptism;
as Christ receives us on earth,
so may he guide us through the trials of this world
and enfold us in the joy of heaven,
where you live and reign,
one God for ever and ever.
Amen.   **P** *1*

¶ The Sending Out

The Blessing

The president may use a seasonal blessing (see items Q2–Q7), or another suitable blessing, or

The God of all grace,
who called you to his eternal glory in Christ Jesus,
establish, strengthen and settle you in the faith;
and the blessing of God almighty,
the Father, the Son, and the Holy Spirit,
be among you and remain with you always.
Amen.   Q *I*

Giving of a Lighted Candle

The president or another person may give each of the newly baptized a lighted candle.

These may be lit from the candle used at the Decision.

When all the newly baptized have received a candle, the president says

God has delivered us from the dominion of darkness
and has given us a place with the saints in light.

You have received the light of Christ;
walk in this light all the days of your life.
**Shine as a light in the world
to the glory of God the Father.**   R *I*

The Dismissal

Go in the light and peace of Christ.
Thanks be to God.   S *I*

Sample 5 – Holy Baptism (incorporating alternative structure options)

In this sample, some of the items (the Signing with the Cross and the Giving of a Lighted Candle) are presented in their alternative *Common Worship* positions. Note that though in this sample service they are both in their alternative position, each item's position can be determined separately. To see all possible options, see the Resource Section of this volume.

If oil is used for the Signing with the Cross in this alternative position, it would normally be the oil of chrism, rather than the oil of baptism.

This sample service is designed to provide the full text needed by the president for a service. The texts used are the standard *Common Worship* forms. Where appropriate, these could be swapped for those provided in the Additional Baptism Texts in Accessible Language.

This sample assumes infant candidates, and so options for candidates who can answer for themselves have been omitted for simplicity.

¶ Preparation

The Greeting

The president says

The grace of our Lord Jesus Christ,
the love of God
and the fellowship of the Holy Spirit be with you all
and also with you. A1

Informal words of welcome or introduction may be said.

Introduction to Baptism

The president may use these or other words

Our Lord Jesus Christ has told us
that to enter the kingdom of heaven
we must be born again of water and the Spirit,
and has given us baptism as the sign and seal of this new birth.
Here we are washed by the Holy Spirit and made clean.
Here we are clothed with Christ,
dying to sin that we may live his risen life.
As children of God,
we have a new dignity and God calls us to fullness of life. C2

The Collect

The president introduces a period of silent prayer with the words 'Let us pray' or a more specific bidding.

Either the Collect of the Day, or this Collect is said

Heavenly Father,
by the power of your Holy Spirit
you give to your faithful people
new life in the water of baptism.
Guide and strengthen us by the same Spirit,
that we who are born again
may serve you in faith and love,
and grow into the full stature of your Son, Jesus Christ,
who is alive and reigns with you
in the unity of the Holy Spirit now and for ever.
Amen.   **D***I*

¶ The Liturgy of the Word

Readings

The readings of the day are normally used on Sundays and Principal Festivals.

Either one or two readings from Scripture may precede the Gospel reading.

At the end of each the reader may say

This is the word of the Lord.
Thanks be to God.   E1

Gospel Reading

When the Gospel is announced the reader says

Hear the Gospel of our Lord Jesus Christ according to N.
Glory to you, O Lord.

At the end

This is the Gospel of the Lord.
Praise to you, O Christ.   E2

Sermon

¶ The Liturgy of Baptism

Presentation of the Candidates

The candidates may be presented to the congregation. Where appropriate, they may be presented by their godparents or sponsors.

The president addresses the whole congregation

Faith is the gift of God to his people.
In baptism the Lord is adding to our number
      those whom he is calling.
People of God,
will you welcome *these children*
and uphold *them* in *their* new life in Christ?
With the help of God, we will.   **F2**

The president then says to the parents and godparents

Parents and godparents, the Church receives *these children* with joy.
Today we are trusting God for *their* growth in faith.
Will you pray for *them*, draw *them* by your example into the community of faith
and walk with *them* in the way of Christ?
With the help of God, we will.

In baptism *these children* begin *their* journey in faith.
You speak for *them* today.
Will you care for *them*, and help *them* to take *their* place
within the life and worship of Christ's Church?
With the help of God, we will.   **F3**

The Decision

A large candle may be lit.

The president addresses the candidates through their parents, godparents and sponsors

In baptism, God calls us out of darkness into his marvellous light.
To follow Christ means dying to sin and rising to new life with him.
Therefore I ask:

Do you reject the devil and all rebellion against God?
I reject them.

Do you renounce the deceit and corruption of evil?
I renounce them.

Do you repent of the sins that separate us from God and neighbour?
I repent of them.

Do you turn to Christ as Saviour?
I turn to Christ.

Do you submit to Christ as Lord?
I submit to Christ.

Do you come to Christ, the way, the truth and the life?
I come to Christ.   G*l*

May almighty God deliver you from the powers of darkness,
restore in you the image of his glory,
and lead you in the light and obedience of Christ.
Amen.   H3

Prayer over the Water

The ministers and candidates gather at the baptismal font.

The president stands before the water of baptism and says (optional seasonal and responsive forms are provided – items 15–19)

Praise God who made heaven and earth,
who keeps his promise for ever.

Let us give thanks to the Lord our God.
It is right to give thanks and praise.   11

We thank you, almighty God, for the gift of water
to sustain, refresh and cleanse all life.
Over water the Holy Spirit moved in the beginning of creation.
Through water you led the children of Israel
from slavery in Egypt to freedom in the Promised Land.
In water your Son Jesus received the baptism of John
and was anointed by the Holy Spirit as the Messiah, the Christ,
to lead us from the death of sin to newness of life.

We thank you, Father, for the water of baptism.
In it we are buried with Christ in his death.
By it we share in his resurrection.
Through it we are reborn by the Holy Spirit.
Therefore, in joyful obedience to your Son,
we baptize into his fellowship those who come to him in faith.

Now sanctify this water that, by the power of your Holy Spirit,
they may be cleansed from sin and born again.
Renewed in your image, may they walk by the light of faith
and continue for ever in the risen life of Jesus Christ our Lord;
to whom with you and the Holy Spirit
be all honour and glory, now and for ever.
Amen.   12

Profession of Faith

The president addresses the congregation

Brothers and sisters, I ask you to profess
together with *these candidates*
the faith of the Church.

Do you believe and trust in God the Father?
I believe in God, the Father almighty,
creator of heaven and earth.

Do you believe and trust in his Son Jesus Christ?
I believe in Jesus Christ, his only Son, our Lord,
who was conceived by the Holy Spirit,
born of the Virgin Mary, suffered under Pontius Pilate,
was crucified, died, and was buried;
he descended to the dead.
On the third day he rose again;
he ascended into heaven,
he is seated at the right hand of the Father,
and he will come to judge the living and the dead.

Do you believe and trust in the Holy Spirit?
I believe in the Holy Spirit,
the holy catholic Church,
the communion of saints,
the forgiveness of sins,
the resurrection of the body,
and the life everlasting.
Amen.   J*1*

Baptism

The president or another minister dips each candidate in water,
or pours water on them, saying

N, I baptize you in the name of the Father,
and of the Son,
and of the Holy Spirit.
Amen.   K2

Signing with the Cross

The president makes the sign of the cross on the forehead of each of the newly baptized, saying

May God, who has received you by baptism into his Church,
pour upon you the riches of his grace,
that within the company of Christ's pilgrim people
you may daily be renewed by his anointing Spirit,
and come to the inheritance of the saints in glory.
Amen. K4

Giving of a Lighted Candle

*The president or another person may give each of the newly baptized
a lighted candle.*

These may be lit from the candle used at the Decision.

When all the newly baptized have received a candle, the president says

God has delivered us from the dominion of darkness
and has given us a place with the saints in light.

You have received the light of Christ;
walk in this light all the days of your life.
**Shine as a light in the world
to the glory of God the Father.** R1

Commission

*A minister addresses the congregation, parents and godparents, using these or
similar words (unless the sermon has already included similar material)*

We have brought *these children* to baptism knowing that Jesus died and
rose again for *them* and trusting in the promise that God hears and
answers prayer. We have prayed that in Jesus Christ *they* will know the
forgiveness of *their* sins and the new life of the Spirit.

As *they grow* up, they will need the help and encouragement of the Christian
community, so that *they* may learn to know God in public worship and
private prayer, follow Jesus Christ in the life of faith, serve *their* neighbour
after the example of Christ, and in due course come to confirmation.

As part of the Church of Christ, we all have a duty to support *them* by prayer, example and teaching. As *their* parents and godparents, you have the prime responsibility for guiding and helping *them* in *their* early years. This is a demanding task for which you will need the help and grace of God.

L*1*

The Welcome

There is one Lord, one faith, one baptism:
N and N, by one Spirit we are all baptized into one body.
We welcome you into the fellowship of faith;
we are children of the same heavenly Father;
we welcome you.

N*1*

The congregation may greet the newly baptized.

The Peace

The president introduces the Peace in these or other suitable words.

(For seasonal Introductions to the Peace, see items N4–N8.)

We are all one in Christ Jesus.
We belong to him through faith,
heirs of the promise of the Spirit of peace.

N2

The peace of the Lord be always with you
and also with you.

A minister may say

Let us offer one another a sign of peace.

All may exchange a sign of peace.

N3

Prayers of Intercession

Intercessions may be led by the president or others.

These or other suitable words may be used

As a royal priesthood, let us pray to the Father
through Christ who ever lives to intercede for us.

Reveal your kingdom among the nations;
may peace abound and justice flourish.
Especially for …

Your name be hallowed.
Your kingdom come.

Send down upon us the gift of the Spirit
and renew your Church with power from on high.
Especially for …

Your name be hallowed.
Your kingdom come.

Deliver the oppressed, strengthen the weak,
heal and restore your creation.
Especially for …

Your name be hallowed.
Your kingdom come.

Rejoicing in the fellowship of the Church on earth,
we join our prayers with all the saints in glory.

Your name be hallowed.
Your kingdom come. **M***l*

The Lord's Prayer

As your children, born again in Christ, we say
Our Father … **M***la*

(For the full text of the Lord's Prayer, see back page.)

¶ The Sending Out

The Blessing

The president may use a seasonal blessing (see items Q2–Q7), or another
suitable blessing, or

The God of all grace,
who called you to his eternal glory in Christ Jesus,
establish, strengthen and settle you in the faith;
and the blessing of God almighty,
the Father, the Son, and the Holy Spirit,
be among you and remain with you always.
Amen.

Q1

The Dismissal

Go in the light and peace of Christ.
Thanks be to God.

S1

Sample 6 – Holy Baptism of those able to answer for themselves (using standard *Common Worship* texts)

This sample draws on material from the standard *Common Worship* service, using the options for the baptism of those able to answer for themselves. The service as laid out here does not include Holy Communion. See Sample 4 for how to adapt the service to include Holy Communion.

¶ Preparation

Greeting

The president says

The grace of our Lord Jesus Christ,
the love of God
and the fellowship of the Holy Spirit be with you all
and also with you. A1

Informal words of welcome or introduction may be said.

Introduction to Baptism

Our Lord Jesus Christ has told us
that to enter the kingdom of heaven
we must be born again of water and the Spirit,
and has given us baptism as the sign and seal of this new birth.
Here we are washed by the Holy Spirit and made clean.
Here we are clothed with Christ,
dying to sin that we may live his risen life.
As children of God, we have a new dignity
and God calls us to fullness of life. C2

The Collect

*The president introduces a period of silent prayer with the words 'Let us pray'
or a more specific bidding.*

*Either the Collect of the Day, or this Collect is said. Seasonal Collects are
also provided.*

Heavenly Father,
by the power of your Holy Spirit
you give your faithful people new life in the water of baptism.
Guide and strengthen us by the same Spirit,
that we who are born again may serve you in faith and love,
and grow into the full stature of your Son, Jesus Christ,
who is alive and reigns with you
in the unity of the Holy Spirit
now and for ever.
Amen.   **D** *1*

¶ The Liturgy of the Word

Readings

Either one or two readings from Scripture may precede the Gospel reading.

At the end of each the reader may say

This is the word of the Lord.
Thanks be to God.   E 1

Gospel Reading

When the Gospel is announced the reader says

Hear the Gospel of our Lord Jesus Christ according to *N*.
Glory to you, O Lord.

At the end

This is the Gospel of the Lord.
Praise to you, O Christ.   E2

Sermon

¶ The Liturgy of Baptism

Presentation of the Candidates

The candidates may be presented to the congregation. Where appropriate they may be presented by their sponsors.

The president asks the candidates for baptism

Do you wish to be baptized?
I do.

Testimony by the candidate(s) may follow.   F1

The president addresses the whole congregation

Faith is the gift of God to his people.
In baptism the Lord is adding to our number
   those whom he is calling.
People of God, will you welcome *these candidates*
and uphold *them* in *their* new life in Christ?
With the help of God, we will.   F2

The Decision

A large candle may be lit.

The president addresses the candidates

In baptism, God calls us out of darkness into his marvellous light.
To follow Christ means dying to sin and rising to new life with him.

Therefore I ask:

Do you reject the devil and all rebellion against God?
I reject them.

Do you renounce the deceit and corruption of evil?
I renounce them.

Do you repent of the sins that separate us from God and neighbour?
I repent of them.

Do you turn to Christ as Saviour?
I turn to Christ.

Do you submit to Christ as Lord?
I submit to Christ.

Do you come to Christ, the way, the truth and the life?
I come to Christ.   G1

The Signing with the Cross

The president or another minister makes the sign of the cross on the forehead of each candidate, saying

Christ claims you for his own.
Receive the sign of his cross.   H1

The president may invite sponsors to sign the candidates with the cross.

When all the candidates have been signed, the president says

Do not be ashamed to confess the faith of Christ crucified.
Fight valiantly as a disciple of Christ
against sin, the world and the devil,
and remain faithful to Christ to the end of your life.   H2

May almighty God deliver you from the powers of darkness,
restore in you the image of his glory,
and lead you in the light and obedience of Christ.
Amen.   H3

Prayer over the Water

The ministers and candidates gather at the baptismal font.

The president stands before the water of baptism and says

Praise God who made heaven and earth,
who keeps his promise for ever.

Let us give thanks to the Lord our God.
It is right to give thanks and praise.   11

We thank you, almighty God, for the gift of water
to sustain, refresh and cleanse all life.
Over water the Holy Spirit moved in the beginning of creation.
Through water you led the children of Israel
from slavery in Egypt to freedom in the Promised Land.
In water your Son Jesus received the baptism of John
and was anointed by the Holy Spirit as the Messiah, the Christ,
to lead us from the death of sin to newness of life.

Lord of life,
renew your creation.

We thank you, Father, for the water of baptism.
In it we are buried with Christ in his death.
By it we share in his resurrection.
Through it we are reborn by the Holy Spirit.
Therefore, in joyful obedience to your Son,
we baptize into his fellowship those who come to him in faith.

Lord of life,
renew your creation.

Now sanctify this water that, by the power of your Holy Spirit,
they may be cleansed from sin and born again.
Renewed in your image, may they walk by the light of faith
and continue for ever in the risen life of Jesus Christ our Lord;
to whom with you and the Holy Spirit
be all honour and glory, now and for ever. Amen.

Lord of life,
renew your creation.   15

Profession of Faith

The president addresses the congregation

Brothers and sisters, I ask you to profess
together with *these candidates*
the faith of the Church.

Do you believe and trust in God the Father?
**I believe in God, the Father almighty,
creator of heaven and earth.**

Do you believe and trust in his Son Jesus Christ?
**I believe in Jesus Christ, his only Son, our Lord,
who was conceived by the Holy Spirit,
born of the Virgin Mary, suffered under Pontius Pilate,
was crucified, died, and was buried;
he descended to the dead.
On the third day he rose again;
he ascended into heaven,
he is seated at the right hand of the Father,
and he will come to judge the living and the dead.**

Do you believe and trust in the Holy Spirit?
**I believe in the Holy Spirit,
the holy catholic Church,
the communion of saints,
the forgiveness of sins,
the resurrection of the body,
and the life everlasting.
Amen.**   J*l*

The president may say to each candidate

N, is this your faith?

Each candidate answers in their own words, or
This is my faith.   **K**1

The president or another minister dips each candidate in water, or pours water on them, saying

N, I baptize you in the name of the Father,
and of the Son,
and of the Holy Spirit.
Amen.   **K**2

If the newly baptized are clothed with a white robe, a hymn or song may be used, and then a minister may say

You have been clothed with Christ.
As many as are baptized into Christ have put on Christ.   **K**3

The president says

May God, who has received you by baptism into his Church,
pour upon you the riches of his grace,
that within the company of Christ's pilgrim people
you may daily be renewed by his anointing Spirit,
and come to the inheritance of the saints in glory.
Amen.   **K**4

The president and those who have been baptized may return from the font.

The Welcome

There is one Lord, one faith, one baptism:
N and N, by one Spirit we are all baptized into one body.
We welcome you into the fellowship of faith;
we are children of the same heavenly Father;
we welcome you. **N**/

The congregation may greet the newly baptized.

The Peace

The president introduces the Peace in these or other suitable words.

We are all one in Christ Jesus.
We belong to him through faith,
heirs of the promise of the Spirit of peace. **N**2

The peace of the Lord be always with you
and also with you.

A minister may say

Let us offer one another a sign of peace.

All may exchange a sign of peace. **N**3

Prayers of Intercession

Intercessions may be led by the president or others. These or other suitable
words may be used.

As a royal priesthood, let us pray to the Father
through Christ who ever lives to intercede for us.

Reveal your kingdom among the nations;
may peace abound and justice flourish.
Especially for …

Your name be hallowed.
Your kingdom come.

Send down upon us the gift of the Spirit
and renew your Church with power from on high.
Especially for …

Your name be hallowed.
Your kingdom come.

Deliver the oppressed, strengthen the weak,
heal and restore your creation.
Especially for …

Your name be hallowed.
Your kingdom come.

Rejoicing in the fellowship of the Church on earth,
we join our prayers with all the saints in glory.

Your name be hallowed.
Your kingdom come.   **M***l*

The Lord's Prayer

The prayers conclude with the Lord's Prayer.

As your children, born again in Christ, we say
Our Father …   **M***l a*

(For the full text of the Lord's Prayer, see back page.)

¶ The Sending Out

Commission

A minister may say to the newly baptized (unless the sermon has included similar material)

Those who are baptized are called to worship and serve God.

Will you continue in the apostles' teaching and fellowship,
in the breaking of bread, and in the prayers?
With the help of God, I will.

Will you persevere in resisting evil,
and, whenever you fall into sin, repent and return to the Lord?
With the help of God, I will.

Will you proclaim by word and example
the good news of God in Christ?
With the help of God, I will.

Will you seek and serve Christ in all people,
loving your neighbour as yourself?
With the help of God, I will.

Will you acknowledge Christ's authority over human society,
by prayer for the world and its leaders,
by defending the weak, and by seeking peace and justice?
With the help of God, I will.

May Christ dwell in your heart(s) through faith,
that you may be rooted and grounded in love
and bring forth the fruit of the Spirit.
Amen.   L3

The Blessing

The president may use a seasonal blessing (see items Q2–Q7), or another suitable blessing, or

The God of all grace,
who called you to his eternal glory in Christ Jesus,
establish, strengthen and settle you in the faith;
and the blessing of God almighty,
the Father, the Son, and the Holy Spirit,
be among you and remain with you always.
Amen.   Q1

Giving of a Lighted Candle

The president or another person may give each of the newly baptized a lighted candle. These may be lit from the candle used at the Decision.

When all the newly baptized have received a candle, the president says

God has delivered us from the dominion of darkness
and has given us a place with the saints in light.

You have received the light of Christ;
walk in this light all the days of your life.
Shine as a light in the world
to the glory of God the Father.   R1

The Dismissal

Go in the light and peace of Christ
Thanks be to God.   S1

Sample 7 – Holy Baptism of those able to answer for themselves (using Additional Baptism Texts in Accessible Language)

This sample draws on material from the Additional Baptism Texts in Accessible Language, demonstrating how these may be used for the baptism of those able to answer for themselves. The alternative form of Profession of Faith (for use when there are strong pastoral reasons) has also been included, and the Presentation of the Candidates has been moved to the earlier position, as part of the Preparation section.

The service as laid out here does not include Holy Communion. See Sample 3 for how to adapt the service to include Holy Communion.

¶ Preparation

Greeting

The president says

The grace of our Lord Jesus Christ,
the love of God
and the fellowship of the Holy Spirit be with you all
and also with you.   A1

Informal words of welcome or introduction may be said.

Introduction to Baptism

Our Lord Jesus Christ has told us
that to enter the kingdom of heaven
we must be born again of water and the Spirit,
and has given us baptism as the sign and seal of this new birth.
Here we are washed by the Holy Spirit and made clean.
Here we are clothed with Christ,
dying to sin that we may live his risen life.
As children of God, we have a new dignity
and God calls us to fullness of life.   C2

Presentation of the Candidates

The candidates may be presented to the congregation. Where appropriate they may be presented by their sponsors.

The president asks those candidates who are able to answer for themselves

Do you wish to be baptized?
I do.

Testimony by the candidate(s) may follow.

The president addresses the whole congregation

We thank God for *N and N* who *have* come to be baptized today.
Christ loves *them* and welcomes *them* into his Church.
Will you support *them* on *their* journey of faith?
We will.   F5

The Collect

The president introduces a period of silent prayer with the words 'Let us pray' or a more specific bidding.

Either the Collect of the Day, or this Collect is said. Seasonal Collects are also provided.

Heavenly Father,
by the power of your Holy Spirit
you give your faithful people new life in the water of baptism.
Guide and strengthen us by the same Spirit,
that we who are born again may serve you in faith and love,
and grow into the full stature of your Son, Jesus Christ,
who is alive and reigns with you
in the unity of the Holy Spirit
now and for ever.
Amen.   D1

¶ The Liturgy of the Word

Readings

Either one or two readings from Scripture may precede the Gospel reading.

At the end of each the reader may say

This is the word of the Lord.
Thanks be to God.   E1

Gospel Reading

When the Gospel is announced the reader says

Hear the Gospel of our Lord Jesus Christ according to *N.*
Glory to you, O Lord.

At the end

This is the Gospel of the Lord.
Praise to you, O Christ.   E2

Sermon

¶ The Liturgy of Baptism

The Decision

A large candle may be lit.

The president addresses the candidates

We all wander far from God and lose our way:
Christ comes to find us and welcomes us home.
In baptism we respond to his call.

Therefore I ask:

Do you turn away from sin?
I do.

Do you reject evil?
I do.

The candidates, together with their sponsors, may turn at this point.

Do you turn to Christ as Saviour?
I do.

Do you trust in him as Lord?
I do.   G2

The Signing with the Cross

The president or another minister makes the sign of the cross on the forehead of each candidate, saying

Christ claims you for his own.
Receive the sign of his cross.   H1

The president may invite sponsors to sign the candidates with the cross.

When all the candidates have been signed, the president says

Do not be ashamed of Christ.
You are his for ever.
Stand bravely with him
against all the powers of evil,
and remain faithful to Christ to the end of your life.   H4

May almighty God deliver you from the powers of darkness,
and lead you in the light and obedience of Christ.
Amen. H5

Prayer over the Water

The ministers and candidates gather at the baptismal font.

The president stands before the water of baptism and says

Praise God who made heaven and earth,
who keeps his promise for ever.

Let us give thanks to the Lord our God.
It is right to give thanks and praise. 11

Loving Father,
we thank you for your servant Moses,
who led your people through the waters of the Red Sea
to freedom in the Promised Land.
We thank you for your Son Jesus,
who has passed through the deep waters of death
and opened for all the way of salvation.
Now send your Spirit,
that those who are washed in this water
may die with Christ and rise with him,
to find true freedom as your children,
alive in Christ for ever.
Amen. 13

Profession of Faith

The president says

Let us affirm,
together with *these who are* being baptized,
our common faith in Jesus Christ.

Do you believe and trust in God the Father,
source of all being and life,
the one for whom we exist?
I believe and trust in him.

Do you believe and trust in God the Son,
who took our human nature,
died for us and rose again?
I believe and trust in him.

Do you believe and trust in God the Holy Spirit,
who gives life to the people of God
and makes Christ known in the world?
I believe and trust in him.

This is the faith of the Church.
This is our faith.
We believe and trust in one God,
Father, Son and Holy Spirit.   J2

Baptism

The president may say to each candidate

N, is this your faith?

Each candidate answers in their own words, or
This is my faith.   K1

The president or another minister dips each candidate in water, or pours water
on them, saying

N, I baptize you in the name of the Father,
and of the Son,
and of the Holy Spirit.
Amen.   K2

If the newly baptized are clothed with a white robe, a hymn or song may be
used, and then a minister may say

You have been clothed with Christ.
As many as are baptized into Christ have put on Christ.   K3

The president says

May God, who has received you by baptism into his Church,
pour upon you the riches of his grace,
that within the company of Christ's pilgrim people
you may daily be renewed by his anointing Spirit,
and come to the inheritance of the saints in glory.
Amen.   K4

The president and those who have been baptized may return from the font.

The Welcome

There is one Lord, one faith, one baptism:
N and N, by one Spirit we are all baptized into one body.
We welcome you into the fellowship of faith;
we are children of the same heavenly Father;
we welcome you.   N1

The congregation may greet the newly baptized.

The Peace

The president introduces the Peace in these or other suitable words.

We are all one in Christ Jesus.
We belong to him through faith,
heirs of the promise of the Spirit of peace.   N2

The peace of the Lord be always with you
and also with you.

A minister may say

Let us offer one another a sign of peace.

All may exchange a sign of peace.   N3

Prayers of Intercession

Intercessions may be led by the president or others.
These or other suitable words may be used.

As a royal priesthood, let us pray to the Father
through Christ who ever lives to intercede for us.

Reveal your kingdom among the nations;
may peace abound and justice flourish.
Especially for …

Your name be hallowed.
Your kingdom come.

Send down upon us the gift of the Spirit
and renew your Church with power from on high.
Especially for …

Your name be hallowed.
Your kingdom come.

Deliver the oppressed, strengthen the weak,
heal and restore your creation.
Especially for …

Your name be hallowed.
Your kingdom come.

Rejoicing in the fellowship of the Church on earth,
we join our prayers with all the saints in glory.

Your name be hallowed.
Your kingdom come.   M *l*

The Lord's Prayer

The prayers conclude with the Lord's Prayer.

As your children, born again in Christ, we say
Our Father …   M *l a*

(For the full text of the Lord's Prayer, see back page.)

¶ The Sending Out

A minister may say to the newly baptized (unless the sermon has included similar material)

Those who are baptized are called to worship and serve God.

Will you continue in the apostles' teaching and fellowship,
in the breaking of bread, and in the prayers?
With the help of God, I will.

Will you persevere in resisting evil,
and, whenever you fall into sin, repent and return to the Lord?
With the help of God, I will.

Will you proclaim by word and example
the good news of God in Christ?
With the help of God, I will.

Will you seek and serve Christ in all people,
loving your neighbour as yourself?
With the help of God, I will.

Will you acknowledge Christ's authority over human society,
by prayer for the world and its leaders,
by defending the weak, and by seeking peace and justice?
With the help of God, I will.

May Christ dwell in your heart(s) through faith,
that you may be rooted and grounded in love
and bring forth the fruit of the Spirit.
Amen.   L3

The Blessing

The president may use a seasonal blessing (see items Q2–Q7), or another
suitable blessing, or

The God of all grace,
who called you to his eternal glory in Christ Jesus,
establish, strengthen and settle you in the faith;
and the blessing of God almighty,
the Father, the Son, and the Holy Spirit,
be among you and remain with you always.
Amen.   Q∕

Giving of a Lighted Candle

The president or another person may give each of the newly baptized
a lighted candle. These may be lit from the candle used at the Decision.

When all the newly baptized have received a candle, the president says

God has delivered us from the dominion of darkness
and has given us a place with the saints in light.

You have received the light of Christ;
walk in this light all the days of your life.
Shine as a light in the world
to the glory of God the Father.   R∕

The Dismissal

Go in the light and peace of Christ
Thanks be to God.   S∕

Guidance notes for particular circumstances

Making baptism services accessible for all

There is good general guidance and advice about making Church life and worship accessible to all, including people with a range of disabilities, on the Church of England website: www.churchofengland.org/more/church-resources/welcoming-disabled-people

This includes the 'A Place to Belong' Guide and 'A Place to Belong' Audit, and links to a range of other resources in print or online.

However, baptism services present particular challenges and opportunities. These guidance notes are focused specifically on issues that relate to baptism services. We are taking for granted here that basic accessibility provision is already in place (for instance, level access to the building and a loop system for hearing aids).

The use of the Additional Baptism Texts in Accessible Language is one obvious way of increasing inclusion for some people and in some contexts. In general, it is good to remember that it is not just children, but a whole range of others, for whom reading large chunks of unfamiliar text is difficult or slow, so don't make assumptions.

Some general principles

Who is affected?

Accessibility is not just important when it is the baptism candidate who has a disability. Remember to think more broadly and to check whether there are any among the parents, godparents and wider family and friends who will be attending who may also have additional needs or for whom aspects of the service or your building might be particularly difficult. The appropriate adjustments will vary depending on who is affected and what part they play in the service.

Preparing in advance

Whatever the disability and whoever is affected, it will always be important to be aware in advance so that any necessary plans can be made. Make sure that early in the process of organizing a baptism service you ask about any additional needs of those who will be involved, whatever their role. Candidates or parents may not think to mention the needs of someone who is part of the wider family but will not be involved in the core baptismal party, so asking the question is important. Perhaps you might develop your own checklist of questions as part of the process of organizing a baptism, to make sure that everyone will feel welcome and included.

A thorough rehearsal in situ will be doubly useful if candidates, parents, godparents or sponsors have disabilities, irrespective of what the particular additional needs are.

Good for some – good for all

Many aspects of a baptism service that make it more engaging and exciting for many can also make it less accessible for some. However, it is also the case that changes that make a service more accessible for some people can also help others too. For instance, making provision for those who cannot easily stand will benefit some people with mobility problems or those who are wheelchair users, but it may also help others who have illnesses or disabilities that affect their energy levels, and someone else who is exhausted and weak because of a course of chemotherapy or other treatment.

Some particular needs

Deaf and deafened people and those who are hard of hearing

Most churches already realize the importance of using a loop system to help hearing-aid users. Baptism services raise particular challenges, including making sure that everyone who is speaking has access to a microphone and can be picked up by the loop system (including candidates, parents, godparents, and sponsors). Baptism services also often include moving to different parts of the church building, such as gathering around the font. Are there microphones there as well, and if you use radio microphones, have you checked the reception when these other parts of the building are used? If you are baptizing by submersion (when using microphones can be practically challenging), how will you ensure that the person baptizing the candidate can be heard?

Those who are Deaf will probably be lip-reading and/or will need a British Sign Language (BSL) interpreter. In either case, it will be important that the lighting is good so that the person speaking and the interpreter can be easily seen. This may not be a problem at the front of the church, but what about if the font is at the back under a balcony or in a corner?

Deaf people need to see in order to know what is happening, and they can't look in two places at once. This can be a particular challenge in baptism services, where actions often accompany words (for instance, pouring water while saying a prayer or giving informal explanations), or words are on a screen or a printed sheet, while action is taking place elsewhere. Make sure you pace things and separate action from speaking to help with this.

The use of visual symbols is particularly helpful for Deaf people, so make the most of those built into the baptism service: water, oil, candles, the sign of the cross. Make sure these symbols don't get lost and that they are not 'talked over'.

Make sure there are clear visual clues, or use touch, to help a Deaf person know what is happening – for instance, a Deaf person leaning over a font for baptism will not necessarily know when the water pouring is finished.

Lip-readers need to be able to see the face of the person who is speaking, so make sure you don't obscure your face or turn away while still speaking. You may need to help others who are involved in the baptism service to be aware of this too. Lip-readers are used to following normal speech at normal speed, so don't be tempted to slow down or to exaggerate your lip movements.

If a BSL/English interpreter is needed, remember that they will need a full text of the service in advance. This is particularly important for a baptism service because it includes even more 'specialist' terms than a normal service. Interpreters will also need the text or notes for the sermon, the Commission, any testimonies being given, the words of any hymns or songs, and the names of all the candidates. Some or all of this may be useful to someone who lip-reads as well, in case there are participants or parts of the service they cannot see clearly.

It is appropriate for a Deaf person (candidate, parent or godparent) to give responses in either BSL or spoken English. Signed responses at any point in the service may take slightly longer than spoken ones, so take account of this before moving on. The Additional Baptism Texts in Accessible Language are often more straightforward for signing, and the simple response by the candidate at the Decision ('I do') is much easier to turn into a strongly affirmative signed 'Amen' or 'Yes'.

People who use BSL cannot sign and hold things at the same time, so make use of screens for the words of the service, or make sure that someone else can hold any order of service for the Deaf person. It is also important that the background behind the interpreter is not too 'busy', so that signs can be clearly seen. This may affect where they stand. The minister might also want to keep any robes as simple as possible, so as not to add distracting 'visual noise'. If there are a significant number of Deaf people in the congregation, they are likely to want to sit near the front, and will not stand for hymns, as those not on the front row will need to be able to see the interpreter.

Make sure you have a run-through rehearsal, at which you can think carefully about where the interpreter should stand at each part of the service (especially important if the font is not at the front of the church). If the candidate and some members of the congregation need an interpreter, you may need two – one to sign for the congregation and one to sign for the candidate – and they may need to stand in different places.

Blind people and those with visual impairment

All the normal advice applies here of course – making sure that service orders and the words for songs and hymns are available in large print or braille as required. If your church relies on screens for the words, make sure that they are available in print form too for those whose distance sight is particularly poor. If you are providing printed sheets for candidates, parents and godparents, these should also be made available to others who may not be able to see a screen easily. Do take advice about what colour of paper to use (or what colour background to use on screen) – for some people with dyslexia and some people with visual difficulties, as well as some people with visual impairment, particular colours can be more or less helpful. As a general rule, use a pale background, but avoid white.

For blind or severely visually-impaired people, the service may need to be sensitively audio-described, at least in part. This might be a combination of someone sitting or standing with them giving a quiet running commentary, and the minister saying clearly what is happening or about to happen.

Make sure someone is available to lead a blind person appropriately if they are moving to the front or to the font. One way of doing this is by walking beside them, offering them your elbow to guide them, but make sure you ask what method they prefer. When they return to their place, you can help a blind person to find their seat by directing their hand to the back of the chair or pew.

Blind people and those with visual impairment may also be literally tripped up by movement which involves steps or changes of floor level – for instance, at the front of the church, or near the font.

Wheelchair users and people with mobility problems

Baptism services usually involve changes in posture, and often involve movement from one part of the building to another, for the baptismal party and sometimes for the whole congregation. Make sure you allow time for those with mobility problems to move, and take account of steps and other changes in floor level. This might mean making changes to which parts of the building are used for which parts of the service.

Remember that wheelchair users (or others who cannot stand) will be lower down than people who are standing up, so make sure that they can see what is going on. We often invite children to come to the front so that they can see a baptism – make sure that there is also provision for wheelchair users to be able to see, not just what is happening at the front of the church, but also at the font or baptism pool. If the words are all on a screen, this can also be hard to see for those who are lower down when others around them are standing.

If the candidate is a wheelchair user, the usual baptismal font may be impossible to use, so consider other options, but where possible keeping a clear connection between this baptism and other baptisms. If a wheelchair user wishes a full immersion baptism then think creatively about other organisations that could help – there may be a local special school or college, or a leisure centre, with a hoist or fully accessible pool which could be used.

People with autism

Some people with autism, or on the autism spectrum, find noisy and busy situations difficult, and can get sensory overload. Remember to take that into consideration when working with a family to consider whether a baptism service should take place in a main Sunday service or as a separate service.

Someone who is on the autistic spectrum will also usually be helped by knowing in advance what is going to happen. If the candidate, or someone else with a key role in the service, is autistic then a rehearsal will be particularly valuable. Anyone who is going to be in the congregation who is on the autism spectrum might value coming in advance to a church building they are not familiar with, to help them to feel more comfortable on the day. Other possibilities include using photographs of the church, the font, the priest (in the robes they will be wearing on the day), candles, oil, and so on. Be as clear as you can about start and finish times, where the person will sit or stand, practical arrangements, posture instructions and so on.

If it is the candidate who has autism, sudden or unexpected action might be frightening, so make sure everything is gently paced and explained or demonstrated in advance. This includes not just what will happen with the water, but also other actions like being signed with the cross, anointed with oil, or given a candle or certificate. If you use chrism oil, don't forget to explain that it has a particular smell.

Many children and adults who are autistic do not like being touched, so make sure you take account of this in planning for the signing of the cross, and any use of oil, as well as arrangements for the baptism itself.

It may also be helpful to provide a specifically designated quieter space in the building – perhaps a side chapel or another part of the building further away from the main action of the baptism.

Think about other aspects of the service too: clapping (and cheering) the newly baptized; flash photography; loud singing or music (including background music as people arrive) can all be problematic for some people. Make sure that there are clear instructions and warnings about what is coming. Camera flashes can be problematic for people with photo-sensitive epilepsy as well, so give clear instructions about when people can take photographs and when they can't so that those affected (for whatever reason) can be prepared.

Using the Holy Baptism service cards

The service cards produced for 'Holy Baptism' and 'Holy Baptism in a Service of Holy Communion' were designed to complement the Additional Baptism Texts in Accessible Language, with an attractive and approachable style and design.

Each card only includes the key texts needed by the congregation, so clergy who are using them need to think carefully about what other resources they will need in order to lead the service (see, for instance, Sample Services 1 and 3 in this book, and the equivalent full texts for the baptism of children in *Common Worship: Baptism and Confirmation* – the Form B services in that volume are the ones that use the Additional Baptism Texts in Accessible Language).

An example in practice

St Cedric's is a town centre church with 40–50 baptisms a year. Families are invited to have the baptism at the 10.00 a.m. Parish Eucharist if they wish, but most choose a separate 'stand-alone' baptism service on a Sunday lunchtime or afternoon, often saying that the main service is too early for their friends and relatives to travel to.

The PCC decided to use the centrally produced 'Holy Baptism' card for these services, as it looks professional and is more long lasting than the previous parish Baptism booklets which they produced themselves. Also, if a family opts for Baptism in the main parish Eucharist, the 'Holy Baptism in a Service of Holy Communion' card can be used to give a consistent parish approach. The vicar and curate miss some of the alternative options they used to print out, but the clarity of the card and the use of the Additional Baptism Texts offer the accessibility they feel is important for the number of people attending who are not regular worshippers. For the extra texts needed by the minister they use the full version of the service in *Common Worship: Baptism and Confirmation* (Baptism of Children outside a main Sunday Service: Form B).

There may be anything from 12 to 120 people invited by the family. One of the parish baptism visitors is on hand to give out the service cards at the door – they will have been to see the family in the previous fortnight to say hello, answer any questions, and find out a bit more about who the godparents are and how many children might be attending. The vicar or curate will have been to visit the family earlier on, soon after the baptism request was first made, and they will have taken a copy of the service card to leave with the family, having talked through the key sections with them. There will also have been a short rehearsal sometime in the week preceding the service.

The 'Getting Ready' section

Before the Greeting, the priest who is leading the service always explains that the service starts at the top of page 1 of the card where it says 'Getting Ready', as the way the cards open up can make this less obvious than opening a service booklet.

The 'Baptizing' section

For the Decision, they always incorporate the option for parents and godparents to turn physically after the first two answers. Experience has shown that this needs to be carefully explained at the baptism visit, and reiterated in the service itself so that the baptism party is reminded, and everyone else understands what is going on.

When they first used the service cards and the Additional Texts, they got the parents and godparents to turn from facing west to facing east, but they found this left them with their backs to the congregation and required further instruction to turn back again. More recently, to keep things simpler, they have the Easter candle to one side at the front of the church and get the parents and godparents to turn to face that. They stay facing it for the Decision and the Signing with the Cross that follows.

At the Signing with the Cross, after the first two sentences ('Christ claims you for his own. Receive the sign of his cross'), the parents and godparents (and any other children of the family) are also invited to make the sign of the cross on the forehead of the child. Then the final words ('Do not be ashamed of Christ. You are his for ever') are added, in order to give people the 'cue' for the congregational words 'Stand bravely with him…'.

Usually the second Prayer over the Water on the card is used, as it refers more immediately to Jesus, although the vicar and curate recognize that in Eastertide the first Prayer over the Water with its opening reference to Moses could be a seasonal option.

Before the responsive Profession of Faith, the vicar or curate always adds some informal words of introduction to explain that because we are baptized 'in the name of the Father and of the Son and of the Holy Spirit', we have a short summary of the Christian faith and its particular understanding of God immediately before the baptism itself.

The responses printed in the card for 'Praying for the World' are for the Ordinary Time prayers of intercession or the Epiphany/Baptism of Christ/Trinity option – but other forms of intercession could use either of these responses. Where appropriate, St Cedric's give the option for one or two of the godparents to join in leading these prayers, or some individual prayers (e.g. prayer L5). These are sent to them in advance.

The 'Going Out' section

As a final announcement, after the service and before the photos start, people are given the opportunity to take the baptism card away with them if they wish, as a reminder of the day and a chance to use the prayers again to pray for the child. Quite a few people take up this offer, which has been expensive for St Cedric's, but the PCC agreed that it was worth it if it helps people to reflect on the service and all it means once they are back at home.

Baptizing adults

Although in the Church of England, baptisms of older children and adults are increasing year on year, most of our guidance and instinctive approach to baptism tends to focus on infants (who still make up the vast majority of baptisms). What follows is some guidance that relates to the particularity of adult candidates.

Support

Candidates who are able to answer for themselves are less likely to have godparents (though they may be included for older children) and more likely to have sponsors.

Confirmation

Canon B 24 requires that the bishop should be informed of any adult baptism at least a week before the baptism takes place, and that the candidate should be confirmed as soon after the baptism as possible. This is clearly most easily accomplished if adults are baptized by the bishop and then confirmed at the same service. Where this is not possible or not the most pastorally appropriate response, it is important that arrangements for confirmation are borne in mind when the baptism is being planned.

A key part of that planning will include making a decision about whether the newly baptized adult will delay their admission to Holy Communion until their confirmation, or whether they will be admitted to Communion on the basis of their baptism, as someone fulfilling the requirement to be 'ready and desirous' to be confirmed (Canon B 15A).

When adult baptisms take place in the context of a confirmation service, the baptisms can take a lot of the attention (especially if they are by immersion). Make sure that any other candidates who are 'only' being confirmed don't end up looking or feeling like their experience is less significant.

Mode of baptism

An infant candidate can be baptized by immersion, and many adults are baptized by having water poured on their head as they lean over the font. However, in practice, an adult baptism is more likely to prompt the question about whether immersion or submersion might be appropriate, and an infant candidate is less likely to prompt that question.

Submersion (or 'full immersion') carries its own practical implications. There needs to be deep enough water – and this is usually provided by means of a baptism pool. In some churches these are built-in, but in most this will mean a portable pool of some sort. Specially designed portable baptism pools are available, but birthing pools have been used, or large inflatable pools designed for summer use in the garden (halfway between a paddling pool and a swimming pool). Some congregations will borrow a neighbouring church which has a built-in baptism pool, or will use a local swimming pool, or a river or the sea.

Practical questions for immersion baptisms

There are a number of practical questions to consider:

- Where will the pool be placed? Here there is sometimes a tension between somewhere that can be seen easily by the congregation, and somewhere that is close enough to any other font to show the connection between the baptism of adults and infants.

- How will the pool be heated? If the pool is to be heated, make sure you use specifically designed portable immersion heaters. It may be that if the pool is to be outdoors, it will not be heated at all.

- Who will do the immersion? Often it will need more than one person, so clergy may be assisted by others (or may delegate the immersion itself to others).

- Where will they be in relation to the pool? It is often assumed that those doing the immersing will be in the pool with the candidate, but it is sometimes possible to stand or kneel outside the pool. This partly depends on how the immersion takes place. The most common approach is to tip the candidate backwards into the water, but other possibilities are worth considering, including having candidates kneel in the water and immersing them by leaning them forwards. Another alternative is to have candidates kneel in the pool and pour copious quantities of water on them.

- How many times will the candidate be immersed? When baptism is by pouring, a threefold application of water alongside the naming of the Trinity is easy. When an adult is being dipped in water and then hauled out of it again, a threefold immersion may be less appropriate (or even possible). This will depend on factors such as the depth of water, size of the candidate, and who is helping. It's important to remember that there is no single 'right' way to do this. *Common Worship* makes clear that a single application of water is perfectly acceptable.

- What will candidates wear for the baptism? Make sure you give clear guidance about appropriate and inappropriate clothing for immersion baptisms – including thinking carefully about what it will look like when wet. Towels will probably need to be at the ready when the newly baptized first emerge from the water.

- What will clergy and assistants wear? Robes can get in the way in the water (and could potentially get dangerous), so if they are worn they need to be as simple as possible (a lightweight cassock alb, for instance, perhaps with small weights in the hem). Other possibilities need to be practical without seeming to trivialize baptism itself.

- Where and when will the newly-baptized get changed? It is important to allow time for getting changed in the flow and structure of the service. Privacy is important in the arrangements for changing, and clergy or other assistants should get changed separately from the candidates. If the newly baptized are to be symbolically clothed in white, dressing gowns or albs could be used. This could be done either immediately following the baptism, or when the newly-baptized arrive back from getting changed, to make a symbol out of a practical necessity.

- Are there particular needs to take into account (see, for instance, the guidance note above on making baptism services accessible)? Baptism, especially (but not only) by immersion, is inherently physical and involves touch and close proximity. When preparing adult candidates (or older children), make sure you are attentive for signs that a candidate may be a survivor of trauma or abuse that may make your normal practices inappropriate or unhelpful, and be ready to respond with flexibility and alternatives.

Particular issues for outdoor baptisms

If baptisms are taking place outdoors (whether in a pool, a river, or the sea) there are particular issues to consider.

The first is the weather – make sure there is a contingency plan for bad weather, including cancelling or postponing if really necessary.

Take account of health and safety in your planning. This will be especially important for baptisms in a river or the sea, where a risk assessment will be essential. Common sense should guide you away from steeply shelving beaches or places where the tides or currents can be strong or unpredictable. The RNLI will be able to give good advice, and should be informed if you are intending to take significant numbers of people into the sea.

It will also be important to think about where the congregation will be in relation to the baptism. A baptism in a narrow river provides a great symbolic opportunity for the candidate to enter the river on one side and come out on the other – but it will be important that the congregation are on the side where the person emerges from the water, ready to receive them into the Church. There are practical issues too. Will the congregation be able to hear above the sound of the wind and/or waves? Will they all be able to see? How will you make sure there is no risk of anyone falling into the water? Will the outdoor venue make it harder for all to be included (see the guidance note above about making baptism services accessible for all)?

Using the Affirmation of Baptismal Faith for individual renewal of baptism

What is Affirmation of Baptismal Faith for?

Many congregations will collectively renew their baptismal vows at significant times in the Church's year, especially at Easter (guidance on how to do this is provided in *Common Worship: Baptism and Confirmation*). When a baptism takes place in the course of regular worship, the congregation may also have the opportunity to be reminded of their baptism, and to be sprinkled with water from the font or to sign themselves with water.

The *Common Worship* service of Affirmation of Baptismal Faith is designed to meet a different and more particular pastoral need. It is provided for individuals who have already been baptized and confirmed, but who now wish to acknowledge a fresh experience of God's grace in their lives in a more public and formal way. This might be because of a sense of taking a significant step forward in faith, or as an act of recommitment (perhaps on returning to the worshipping community after a time of absence), or after a significant or difficult life experience. It can be particularly useful when someone baptized and confirmed as a young person wishes to make a declaration of faith as an adult.

The form provided allows for a vivid recognition of experiences of personal renewal and commitment after baptism and confirmation, and the option for water to be used allows for a strong ritual sign without it looking like a second baptism. It is therefore important to find imaginative and profound ways in which water can be used, while making clear that the water is pointing back to an earlier baptism. As with baptism itself, there is an opportunity to use lots of water, symbolizing the generosity of God and the super-abundance of God's life-giving gifts.

When can it take place?

Affirmation of Baptismal Faith can be incorporated into a service led by the bishop (such as a baptism or confirmation service) but it can also be used as part of the regular worship of a parish, led by the parish clergy. It could happen as part of a baptism service, or on its own.

Key practical tips

The option for water to be used as part of the affirmation service helpfully makes the connection with baptism clear, but it needs to be handled carefully to avoid any confusion with an actual baptism.

- Keep terminology clear throughout the service – this is an affirmation of baptismal faith (which makes clear that a valid baptism has already taken place) rather than a 're-baptism' or a renewal of vows.

- When the water is used, avoid using any form of Trinitarian words that might sound like the words used at baptism.

- Think carefully about how the water is used and who applies it – there might be value in it not being the ordained minister. This will particularly be the case if the person affirming their baptism wishes to do so by full or partial immersion in water.

Some examples of practice

St David's

At St David's the worship committee have looked at how to use water at services of affirmation. They have seen that at St Helen's, the parish next door, they have a small brass bucket and a special brass sprinkler (which they call an *aspergilium*), but at St David's they have experimented with a number of different options, depending on the circumstances. One successful option has been to use a small branch from an evergreen tree or a rosemary plant, which can be dipped in the font and used to sprinkle the person affirming their baptismal faith. They used this when Frank, a retired engineer, asked to affirm his baptismal faith after he had joined a home group for the first time. He found that the chance to talk openly about his faith and to discuss the Bible with others had brought his faith alive in a new way.

At one service, a young person who had been baptized as a child and confirmed as a teenager had returned to Church and wanted to declare her re-found faith as an adult. The worship committee suggested that everyone should gather around the font, which would be filled with water, as at a baptism, full nearly to the brim. After the person had made the Profession of Faith, the Vicar invited her to dip her hand in the water of the font and to trace a small cross on her forehead with the water. The Vicar reminded her and the rest of the congregation that by this small, intimate but powerful gesture she would symbolically retrace the cross that had been traced on her forehead at her baptism, publicly marking her own acceptance of her baptism and the cross. After the service, she commented on how that moment had been both personal and also symbolic of her inclusion in something much greater.

Holy Trinity

Holy Trinity has a significant ministry among teenagers and young adults. Every year they have a number of young people who ask to be baptized, and their evening services of adult baptism are joyful and emotional occasions. A large inflatable baptismal pool is used, which makes baptism by submersion possible. This is set up at the back of the church near the font. Though it makes the logistics complicated (because most of the words for songs and spoken prayers are normally projected on a screen at the front), the ministry team are keen to make clear that infants baptized at the font and adults baptized in the pool are all receiving the same baptism into Christ.

Among the young people asking for 'baptism by full immersion', there are often one or two who turn out to have already been baptized as infants and confirmed as young adolescents, and the vicar has to explain that they cannot be baptized again. The Affirmation of Baptismal Faith is used to enable these young people to affirm that God's involvement in their life through their infant baptism is now finding its fulfilment in their adult faith. Where immersion is very important to them as a sign of the significance of the step of commitment they are taking, they are invited to use the baptismal pool for this.

The vicar and the youth minister have taken great care to think through how to make it clear that this is not a 're-baptism'. Early in the service, when all the candidates are introduced, they are careful to explain the difference between those being baptized and those affirming their baptismal faith. After the baptisms have taken place, the vicar gets out of the baptism pool (where she and the youth minister have been performing the immersion baptisms). Standing at the side of the pool she uses the words of the Declaration from the Affirmation of Baptismal Faith. She then says to the person affirming their baptismal faith: 'N, I invite you to be drenched in the love of God, the God who has loved you since before your baptism, and has been faithful to you since.' The candidate then gets into the baptismal pool, kneels in the water, and the youth minister pours bucketfuls of water over them.

Scenarios

Scenario 1 – St Wilfrid's

Setting the scene

St Wilfrid's is a rural church in a multi-parish benefice. The community around St Wilfrid's is around 150 people, scattered across a number of farms and other rural businesses, many of which have been in the same families for generations. This is a community that consists predominantly of farming families, rather than commuters, those who have retired or those who own second homes in the village.

The church would describe itself as 'ordinary'. For a small community their usual Sunday attendance is good – around 18–20 people. The church is in a field some three hundred yards from the road, and has no water supply, no toilet and no PA system. It is held in great affection by members of the community. The big events of Harvest and Christmas can see 90–100 in attendance.

While the church seats about 100 people, the space inside is limited. The present generation of new parents is traditional in its idea of what Church 'should be like'. They are proud to be the next generation in a long line to farm the land, and baptisms and weddings inevitably include a 'looking up of family' in the graveyard.

Notes on the service

For practical reasons, most infant baptisms at St Wilfrid's take place outside the main Sunday service, because space in the church building is so limited. Baptisms usually take place immediately after the main morning service. The regular congregation are encouraged to stay, and often many of them know the family anyway.

Though this service is a 'stand-alone' baptism, many of the ideas and emphases would work just as well in a main Sunday service in this kind of rural context.

Daniel, who is being baptized in this service, is the first child of one of the couples who live in the village. One set of Daniel's grandparents also live in the village, and the family has been farming in the area for several generations.

General assumptions

This service makes the following assumptions for this context:

- There is not usually accompanied singing at baptisms outside a main service, although this could be arranged.
- Ease of use has been a key factor in the choices made. For example, the accessible language texts and a responsive form of the Profession of Faith are used.
- The Signing with the Cross is done in the alternative position, immediately after the baptism, rather than as part of the Decision. This reflects part of the 'tradition' that is expected here.
- Movement is kept to a minimum due to lack of space in a relatively small building – especially at the front of the nave and round the font.
- At various points the service includes the involvement of an 'elder-figure'. At St Wilfrid's this is usually a member of the grandparents' generation, preferably one who is a member of the regular congregation (for instance, it could be a churchwarden). In this service, the elder-figure is Arthur, one of Daniel's grandparents and a PCC member.

Though the service has a rural farming community in mind, some of the ideas would work in any community where a number of generations still live in the same few square miles – for instance, certain urban areas.

Themes

Using themes of creation and the agricultural year can make links for those attending baptisms whose usual engagement with the Church is at harvest time. The service includes ideas for using material from *Common Worship: Times and Seasons*. Without it being laboured, this approach can create echoes of what is familiar and could be introduced at the following places: the Prayer of Thanksgiving; introduction to baptism; collect; readings; intercessions; songs; blessing. The words in this service have been chosen with this in mind.

A further theme in this context is the importance of the community and generations of family still in one place. This theme can be drawn out in the Introduction before the Thanksgiving Prayer, in the presentation of the candidate and in the role that 'elders' of the family and community play in the service.

Hymn/song ideas

- People will often have 'family hymns' they might like sung.
- In this context, material with a harvest or creation theme and baptismal echoes works well. For instance, 'Great is thy faithfulness' or 'For the beauty of the earth'.
- In the service below, a refrain is used at certain points. The chorus of 'We plough the fields and scatter' is a good one for this, both for its words and for the fact that it may be well known and confidently sung unaccompanied, without the need for printed words. To use a refrain at certain points is a good way of gathering people's attention and bringing them together, such as after the return from the font. In this scenario it is also used instead of the opening dialogue in the Prayer over the Water, as a way of calling the congregation to give thanks.

Prayer of Thanksgiving for the child

The introduction to this part of the service often includes using the parish registers to find parents, grandparents, other relatives and recurring names. A family christening gown is used less often these days, but if it is, then the story of it may be told here. The emphasis here should be on thanksgiving for the new addition to the family, saving comments more specific to coming for baptism for the Presentation. The thanksgiving, introduction and prayers could be led by the elder-figure.

Presentation of the Candidate

Generally the vicar presents the candidate for baptism drawing on conversations she has had with the parents, but she always invites parents to say something themselves if they wish to.

Decision

The parents and godparents are invited to stand in a semi-circle behind the Easter candle, facing the congregation. When they are in situ the candle is lit by the elder-figure.

At the font

A parent, an older child, or another family member, is usually invited to pour the water.

The Prayer over the Water is one of the responsive forms. The 'cue line' ('Lord of life') could be led by the elder-figure or by an older child in the family (with suitable preparation).

Commission and Intercessions

These sections could involve the elder-figure.

Welcome

At St Wilfrid's the parents and child stand in the aisle in the middle of the congregation and everyone stands and turns to face them. The Welcome is held back to this point in the service so that the remainder of the service can happen with them in this position. The Welcome concludes with an encouragement to greet the newly baptized with applause, but the Peace is not shared, as this is not familiar to most families, and the space constraints of the building make it hard to move around.

The Lord's Prayer

The traditional form of the Lord's Prayer is used in baptisms at St Wilfrid's, as it is the version most likely to be known by the majority of all ages in this context, but it is always printed in full, as many younger people no longer know any version by heart.

Giving of a Lighted Candle

If the elder-figure lit the Easter candle at the Decision, the same person lights a candle from it and brings it to the child, giving it to one of the parents

The Service

Preparation

The vicar gives a welcome, and any necessary notices.

Introduction to the Thanksgiving Prayer

Daniel and his parents stand with the vicar, who says

We rejoice today with Daniel's family
as they thank God for the gift of life
and bring him for baptism.

So, let us pray, as we give thanks to God for Daniel,
and pray for his parents.

adapted from **B**1

Thanksgiving Prayer for a Child

Arthur, one of Daniel's grandparents, says this prayer

God our Creator,
we thank you for the wonder of new life
and for the mystery of human love.
We give thanks for all whose support and skill
surround and sustain the beginning of life.
As Jesus knew love and discipline within a human family,
may Daniel grow in strength and wisdom.
As Mary knew the joys and pains of motherhood,
give Daniel's parents your sustaining grace and love;
through Jesus Christ our Lord.
Amen.   **B**2

*This refrain (from the hymn 'We plough the fields and scatter') is
sung together. During the singing, Daniel and his parents return to
their places.*

**All good gifts around us are sent from heaven above;
then thank the Lord, O thank the Lord,
for all his love.**

Introduction to Baptism

The vicar says

God raised Jesus Christ from the dead
and sent the Holy Spirit to recall the whole world to himself.
In baptism we die to sin and rise to newness of life in Christ.
Here we find rebirth in the Spirit,
and set our minds on his heavenly gifts.
As children of God, we are continually created anew,
as we walk the path of faith,
and feed on the forgiveness of his healing grace.   **C**4

The Collect Prayer

The vicar introduces a period of silent prayer, which concludes
with this prayer

Lord of all time and eternity,
you opened heaven's gate and revealed yourself as Father
by the voice that called Jesus your beloved Son,
baptizing him, in the power of the Spirit:
reveal yourself to us now, to claim us as your children,
and so complete the heavenly work of our rebirth
in the waters of the new creation;
through Jesus Christ your Son our Lord,
who is alive and reigns with you, in the unity of the Holy Spirit,
one God, now and for ever.
Amen.   **D**2

The Liturgy of the Word

There is a reading from the Bible, followed by a short address.

The Liturgy of Baptism

Presentation

Daniel is brought to the front by his parents and godparents.

The vicar addresses the whole congregation

Jesus said, 'Let the children come to me. Do not stop them'.
We thank God for Daniel who has come to be baptized today.
Christ loves him and welcomes him into his Church.

So I ask you all:
Will you support Daniel as he begins his journey of faith?
We will.
Will you help him to live and grow within God's family?
We will.

The vicar then addresses the parents and godparents

God knows each of us by name and we are his.
Parents and godparents, you speak for Daniel today.
Will you pray for him, and help him to follow Christ?
We will.   F4

The Decision

Daniel, his parents, and his godparents gather around the Easter candle.
The candle is lit by Arthur.

The vicar addresses Daniel through his parents and godparents

We all wander far from God and lose our way:
Christ comes to find us and welcomes us home.
In baptism we respond to his call.

Therefore I ask:
Do you turn away from sin?
I do.
Do you reject evil?
I do.
Do you turn to Christ as Saviour?
I do.
Do you trust in him as Lord?
I do.   G2

The vicar says

May almighty God deliver you from the powers of darkness,
and lead you in the light and obedience of Christ.
Amen.   **H**5

Prayer over the Water

Daniel, his parents, and his godparents gather at the font. Everyone else turns to face it.

This refrain is sung together

**All good gifts around us are sent from heaven above;
then thank the Lord, O thank the Lord,
for all his love.**

The vicar leads the Prayer over the Water

We thank you, almighty God, for the gift of water
to sustain, refresh and cleanse all life.
Over water the Holy Spirit moved in the beginning of creation.
Through water you led the children of Israel
from slavery in Egypt to freedom in the Promised Land.
In water your Son Jesus received the baptism of John
and was anointed by the Holy Spirit as the Messiah, the Christ,
to lead us from the death of sin to newness of life.

Lord of life,
renew your creation.

We thank you, Father, for the water of baptism.
In it we are buried with Christ in his death.
By it we share in his resurrection.
Through it we are reborn by the Holy Spirit.
Therefore, in joyful obedience to your Son,
we baptize into his fellowship those who come to him in faith.

Lord of life,
renew your creation.

Now sanctify this water that, by the power of your Holy Spirit,
they may be cleansed from sin and born again.
Renewed in your image, may they walk by the light of faith
and continue for ever in the risen life of Jesus Christ our Lord;
to whom with you and the Holy Spirit
be all honour and glory, now and for ever. Amen.

Lord of life,
renew your creation.   I5

Profession of Faith

The vicar addresses everyone

Let us affirm,
together with Daniel, who is being baptized,
our common faith in Jesus Christ.

Do you believe and trust in God the Father,
source of all being and life,
the one for whom we exist?
I believe and trust in him.

Do you believe and trust in God the Son,
who took our human nature,
died for us and rose again?
I believe and trust in him.

Do you believe and trust in God the Holy Spirit,
who gives life to the people of God
and makes Christ known in the world?
I believe and trust in him.

This is the faith of the Church.
This is our faith.
We believe and trust in one God,
Father, Son and Holy Spirit.   J2

Baptism

The vicar baptizes Daniel in water, saying

Daniel Reuben, I baptize you in the name of the Father,
and of the Son,
and of the Holy Spirit.
Amen.   K2

Signing with the Cross

The vicar makes the sign of the cross on Daniel's forehead, saying

May God, who has received you by baptism into his Church,
pour upon you the riches of his grace,
that within the company of Christ's pilgrim people
you may daily be renewed by his anointing Spirit,
and come to the inheritance of the saints in glory.
Amen.   K4

*Everyone turns to face the front, and Daniel, his parents,
and his godparents return to their seats.*

This refrain is sung together as they move

**All good gifts around us are sent from heaven above;
then thank the Lord, O thank the Lord,
for all his love.**

Commission

*The vicar addresses the congregation and Daniel's parents and
godparents using words based on item L2.*

Prayers of Intercession

*A member of St Wilfrid's congregation leads prayers for this community
and for the world. These prayers include the following*

Lord of creation,
you have created the universe by your eternal Word,
and have blessed humanity in giving us dominion over the earth:
we pray for the world,
that we may honour and share its resources,
and live in reverence for the creation
and in harmony with one another.

God of all creation,
receive our prayer.

Your Son has promised that the Spirit will lead us into all truth:
we pray for this community in which you have set us,
for one another and for ourselves,
that we may bring forth the fruit of the Spirit
in love and joy and peace.

God of all creation,
receive our prayer.

You have given your people a rich land,
yet by sin we have made a world of suffering and sorrow:
we pray for those who bear the weight of affliction,
that they may come to share the life of wholeness and plenty.

God of all creation,
receive our prayer.

Your Son Jesus Christ is the first-fruits of the resurrection
and will reap the harvest of the dead at the end of time:
we pray that he will gather us all together
with those who have gone before
in the banquet of the age to come.

God of all creation,
receive our prayer.

Source of all life
and giver of all that is good,
hear our prayers and grant us all that is in accordance with your will;
through Jesus Christ our Lord.
Amen.

> *adapted from* CW: Times and Seasons, *Harvest Intercessions H2*

Welcome

*Daniel is brought to the middle of the congregation,
and all turn to face him.*

The vicar says

There is one Lord, one faith, one baptism:
Daniel, by one Spirit we are all baptized into one body.
**We welcome you into the fellowship of faith;
we are children of the same heavenly Father;
we welcome you.** N1

The vicar invites everyone to greet Daniel with applause.

The Lord's Prayer

In baptism God declares that we are his children, whom he loves;
so let us pray   **M**3a

Our Father, who art in heaven,
hallowed be thy name;
thy kingdom come;
thy will be done;
on earth as it is in heaven.
Give us this day our daily bread.
And forgive us our trespasses,
as we forgive those who trespass against us.
And lead us not into temptation;
but deliver us from evil.
For thine is the kingdom,
the power and the glory,
for ever and ever. Amen.

The Sending Out

The Blessing

May God our Creator,
who clothes the lilies and feeds the birds of the air,
bestow on you his care
and increase the harvest of your righteousness;
and the blessing of God almighty,
the Father, the Son, and the Holy Spirit,
be among you and remain with you always.
Amen.

CW: Times and Seasons, Harvest Blessing P1

Giving of a Lighted Candle

Arthur gives Daniel a lighted candle.

The vicar says

God has delivered us from the dominion of darkness
and has given us a place with the saints in light.

You have received the light of Christ;
walk in this light all the days of your life.
**Shine as a light in the world
to the glory of God the Father.**   **R**1

This refrain is sung together

**All good gifts around us are sent from heaven above;
then thank the Lord, O thank the Lord,
for all his love.**

The Dismissal

Go in the light and peace of Christ.
Thanks be to God.   **S**1

Scenario 2 – St Ethelburga's

Setting the scene

St Ethelburga's has been running a Messy Church one Sunday a month at 4.00 p.m. for four years. The parish consists of a large village which has a pub, a primary school and a Post Office (in a small convenience store). Most of the churchgoers would be hard pushed to give themselves more of a label than 'We're CofE, aren't we?' but the flavour of the music (rendered on organ, keyboard, bass guitar and cello) and the easy-going nature of the leaders (who are known by first names without a title) might lead a visitor to describe them as low to middling.

Maisie, a lone parent and faithful member of Messy Church, has asked the vicar about baptism for herself, her ten-year-old son Jack and her new baby, Honey. She was given the choice of which service to have the baptism in and decided that as Messy Church is her church, it should be there. The vicar and the Messy Church leader, Jill, managed a lively session of baptism preparation with Maisie and her children, in which all of them contributed robustly to the service plans. Maisie decided to make a baptism cake for everyone to share at teatime, and when the vicar said it would be quite a party, she decided to prepare party bags too, to distribute at the end. Both the Messy Church congregation and the congregation from the Sunday morning Parish Communion have been invited.

Maisie has asked Jill to be her sponsor, and to be one of Jack and Honey's godparents, along with some members of her wider family.

Notes on the service

Activity time

The activity time is used to cover the parts of the service which comprise the Liturgy of the Word, and also to prepare things which can be used during the Liturgy of Baptism (such as the Profession of Faith).

The activities in this service are just suggestions that would allow the congregation to explore the themes mentioned in the *Common Worship* Pastoral Introduction: the cross, water, death and new life, Jesus' baptism, light. They include guidance for the leader about how to facilitate conversation as the activity happens.

Helping the congregation to join in

Some parts of the service need the congregation to have words to join in with. In some contexts it may be worth having those words on a screen or a service sheet, but at St Ethelburga's Messy Church they have too high a proportion of pre-readers to make written words helpful. The way that they handle this is to appoint someone as a 'congregation leader' (in some traditions this would be a role for a 'liturgical deacon'). The congregation are told that this person will lead them with their words – whenever this person says something, they all repeat it back, as loudly as they can.

Maisie and Jack will also have things to say in answer to some of the questions, and this will be written down for them. They will have had a rehearsal, but Jill, as Maisie's sponsor, will also be with them and can quietly remind them what to say, if necessary.

Presentation of the Candidates

The form of Presentation used is Option 1 (the standard *Common Worship* form). This is because it flows more easily in situations where there are candidates who cannot answer for themselves as well as those who can.

The Decision

In this service the hinge point in the questions, between turning from evil and turning to Christ, is marked by using one of the earlier activities. At other baptisms at St Ethelburga's they tried something different to mark that transition. The lights were turned off at the start of the questions, and at the point after the first two questions a large lit candle was brought from the back of the church to the front and placed next to the candidate. The lights were turned on again after the answers to the second two questions.

The place of baptism

In this service we've assumed that the service (or at least the Liturgy of Baptism part of it) is taking place in the church building and at the font. However, if it were all taking place in a church hall or other building, or if a paddling pool or baptism pool were being used, it would be important to make sure the portable font or pool was placed somewhere where people can see clearly, but also somewhere to which people have to move, so that the sense of journeying to baptism is enhanced.

Prayer over the Water

In this scenario we've used one of the responsive forms of prayer, where the regular response can be 'cued' in by an older child, and everyone can call out the response each time. An alternative would be to use one of the shorter prayers from the Additional Texts in Accessible Language (items I3 and I4).

The Service

Preparation

The Greeting

Practical announcements are made, and the vicar welcomes everyone using these or similar words

Hello everyone, and welcome to a very special Messy Church.

Today Maisie, Jack and Honey are going to be baptized – or 'christened' as we sometimes call it – and we're going to be finding out with them what baptism is all about.

We give a special welcome to anyone who is here for the first time, and to those who normally come to the Sunday morning Parish Communion service.

We're going to have an hour of activities for everyone to enjoy, to think about what baptism is. If you aren't sure what to do, just ask one of the leaders – anyone with a badge on.

After that, we'll come together for the baptism itself, and then we'll all have tea together.

Activity time – The Liturgy of the Word

The Collect, readings, sermon, Profession of Faith and intercessions are experienced within the hour of ten different activities.

Collect prayer activity

People are invited to make the best prayer possible by rearranging cards with words printed on them. The cards could be laid on a table or pegged to a clothesline. Some cards are left blank for people's own suggestions to be written on.

The cards are laid out in blocks, reflecting the structure of a collect prayer:

1) **Which of these ways do you want to start your prayer?** (Amazing God, / Dear God our Father, / Awesome God, / God of all creation, / *Your own suggestion*)

2) **Which of these things do you want to thank God for most today?** (You brought Jesus back to life. / You created life out of nothing at the start of the world. / You breathe life into things which look dead. / *Your own suggestion*)

3) **What would you most like to ask God to do in today's baptism service?** (Please bring us closer to you today. / Please help Maisie, Jack and Honey to know your love for them today. / Please make today part of the new start we all need. / *Your own suggestion*)

4) **How do you want to 'sign off'?** (We know you and trust you for all this. Amen. / Thank you, amazing God. Amen. / We ask this in the name of Jesus. Amen. / *Your own suggestion*)

Water play

Free play with a baby bath, paddling pool or water play set, with bottles, floating things and sinking things.

What do you use water for each day? Can you think of any Bible stories with water in them?

Water painting

Squirting water from bottles onto a wall or path to write a word to do with water (life, thirst, plants, growth, wash, clean...)

Can you think why we might use water for baptism when it's such an everyday thing but baptism only happens once in someone's life?

Water rockets

For information on this activity, see 'Messy Church Does Science', Chapter 1.

What helps your faith 'fly'? How do you think being baptized today will help Maisie, Jack and Honey's faith to 'fly'?

Cleaning pennies

For information on this activity, see 'Messy Church Does Science', Chapter 9. Maisie, Jack and Honey do NOT do this activity, as they will do it later.

Maisie, Jack and Honey will be making a new, sparkling start today and having anything that stops them sparkling washed away. Do you feel like the 'before' pennies or the 'after' pennies?

Colouring in the scene

Have a big art outline of the scene of Jesus's baptism to paint in.

Tell the story of the picture from Matthew 3.13-17

I wonder why Jesus asked John to baptize him?
What do you think?

Crossing the Red Sea competition

Use clockwork toys and a wide strip of blue card. Each person has to try to get their toy across the Red Sea before the Egyptian soldier toy can get from the pyramid to the water's edge.

Talk about the way the people of God passed through water from slavery or death at the hands of the soldiers on one side to new life in the Promised Land on the other.

Death to life sorting

Have a large cross and a selection of pictures of things, or actual things, that are either dead or alive. (Don't kill anything, of course, and treat living things with respect. Live worms, ants, minibeasts, plants and dead leaves, fossils or coral would work well.)

People are invited to put the dead things on one side of a cross and the live things on the other.

Talk about the difference between life and death. Talk about the way Jesus' cross and resurrection changed death to life and how baptism is a sign of that strange but exciting journey from death to life.

Intercession activity

This involves making a prayer card for Maisie, Jack and Honey.

Each person is invited to write or draw a prayer for them on a heart shape and glue it onto a cross shape on the greetings card.

What would you love God to give Maisie, Jack and Honey to help them follow him more closely in their lives ahead?

Profession of Faith activity

The questions from the alternative responsive form of the Profession of Faith (J2 – see below) are printed out in large print with plenty of space under each one. Sealing-wax sticks are provided in different colours and a variety of different seals/stamps.

The leader invites people to melt a blob of wax in the space under each of the questions and stamp their seal in it, to show that they believe and trust in this God. (Risk assessments are carried out, especially where live flames are involved.)

Do you believe and trust in God the Father, source of all being and life, the one for whom we exist?

Do you believe and trust in God the Son, who took our human nature, died for us and rose again?

Do you believe and trust in God the Holy Spirit, who gives life to the people of God and makes Christ known in the world?

based on **J2**

Talk about how important it is to be real with God about what we believe.

Celebration time – The Liturgy of Baptism

The next section is the part where everyone gathers together. Some of the activities done previously will be used or revisited to connect the two sections.

Gathering song

Chosen by Maisie.

Introduction to Baptism

All our activities today had something to do with baptism. I wonder what we have learned or been reminded of about baptism today?

The vicar and Jill work together, welcoming ideas from the congregation and making sure the key points in the Common Worship Introduction are celebrated.

Presentation of the Candidates

Jill brings Maisie, Jack and Honey to the front (along with the other godparents) and says something like this

There are three people getting baptized today, Maisie, Jack and Honey – and here they all are. In case you haven't met them before, this is Maisie, this is Jack and this is Honey.

Then the vicar asks the formal question

Maisie and Jack, do you wish to be baptized?

They respond, one after the other

I do.   **F**1

Then Jill asks Maisie and Jack to tell everyone a bit about why they've decided to be baptized. Jack reads out the short piece that he has written. Maisie explains without the need for notes.

Jill also asks Maisie why she's chosen to have Honey baptized, and about the name she chose and what it means to her, etc.

The vicar then says to everyone

Faith is the gift of God to his people.
In baptism the Lord is adding to our number
   those whom he is calling.
People of God, will you welcome Maisie, Jack and Honey
and uphold them in their new life in Christ?

Led by the congregation leader, everyone responds

With the help of God, we will.
With the help of God, we will. *adapted from* **F2**

The vicar then says to Maisie and to the godparents of Jack and Honey

The Church receives Jack and Honey with joy.
Today we are trusting God for their growth in faith.
Will you pray for them,
draw them by your example into the community of faith
and walk with them in the way of Christ?
With the help of God, we will.

In baptism Jack and Honey begin their journey in faith.
You speak for them today.
Will you care for them,
and help them to take their place
within the life and worship of Christ's Church?
With the help of God, we will. **F3**

The Decision

The vicar says something like this

I've got some important questions to ask Maisie and Jack now.
Maisie is going to be answering for Jack and Honey too, and so are
their godparents.

Maisie, Jack and Honey,
we all wander far from God and lose our way:
Christ comes to find us and welcomes us home.
In baptism we respond to his call.

Therefore I ask:

Do you turn away from sin?
I do.
Do you reject evil?
I do.

At this point, Maisie, Jack and Honey are invited to do the 'Cleaning pennies' activity, and the godparents help out. While this is happening, Jill gives some words of explanation, reminding everyone about when they did this activity, and connecting it with the decision to follow Christ that Maisie, Jack and Honey are making.

When they have each cleaned a penny, the vicar continues

Do you turn to Christ as Saviour?
I do.
Do you trust in him as Lord?
I do.   **G**2

Signing with the Cross

Jill makes the sign of the cross on the foreheads of Maisie, Jack and Honey, and then invites Maisie and the godparents to do the same for Jack and Honey.

Jill uses these words as she makes the sign of the cross (reassuring the others that they don't need to worry about the words, but just make the sign).

Maisie / Jack / Honey, Christ claims you for his own.
Receive the sign of his cross.   **H**1

When they have all been signed, the vicar says

Do not be ashamed of Christ.
You are his for ever.

Stand bravely with him
Stand bravely with him

against all the powers of evil,
against all the powers of evil,

and remain faithful to Christ to the end of your life.
and remain faithful to Christ to the end of your life.　　　　　H4

The vicar continues

May almighty God deliver you from the powers of darkness,
and lead you in the light and obedience of Christ.

Led by the congregation leader, everyone responds

Amen.
Amen.　　　　　H5

Prayer over the Water

Everybody moves to gather at the font.

Maisie, Jack, and Honey, along with Jill and the other godparents, all stand behind the font with the vicar. Everyone else gathers round. The vicar invites children, and anyone else who can't see, to move to the front or somewhere else where they can see more easily.

The congregation leader leads the opening dialogue.

While this is happening, children and some other congregation members are each given a cup of warm water with which they are invited to help fill the font.

Praise God,
Praise God,

who made heaven and earth,
who made heaven and earth,

who keeps his promise for ever.
who keeps his promise for ever.

Let's give thanks to God.
Let's give thanks to God.

Let's give our thanks and praise.
Let's give our thanks and praise.

adapted from I1

In the prayer that follows, the congregation leader says 'Saving God, give us life' each time and everyone repeats it.

While the prayer is being said, one of the activity leaders holds up the coloured-in artwork depicting Jesus's baptism.

Almighty God, whose Son Jesus Christ
was baptized in the river Jordan,
we thank you for the gift of water
to cleanse us and revive us.

Saving God, give us life.
Saving God, give us life.

We thank you that through the waters of the Red Sea
you led your people out of slavery
to freedom in the Promised Land.

Saving God, give us life.
Saving God, give us life.

We thank you that through the deep waters of death
        you brought your Son,
and raised him to life in triumph.

Saving God, give us life.
Saving God, give us life.

Bless this water, that your servants who are washed in it
may be made one with Christ in his death and in his resurrection,
to be cleansed and delivered from all sin.

Saving God, give us life.
Saving God, give us life.

Send your Holy Spirit upon them,
bring them to new birth in the household of faith
and raise them with Christ to full and eternal life;
for all might, majesty, authority and power are yours,
now and for ever. Amen.

Saving God, give us life.
Saving God, give us life.

adapted from 18

Profession of Faith

One of the activity leaders brings the Profession of Faith activity sheets, with everyone's wax stamp on, to the font now and lifts it up so that everyone can see it.

The vicar says something like this

Earlier, in our activity time, we had the chance to think about what we believe about God the Father, about Jesus and about the Holy Spirit, and how we trust in God. In baptism, Maisie, Jack and Honey are going to be baptized into this faith, this Christian way of understanding God. It's an understanding that they will be sharing with us and with the Christian Church all over the world and in every age.

So let's agree together that this is our faith:
This is the faith of the Church.

Led by the congregation leader, everyone responds

This is our faith.
This is our faith.
We believe and trust in one God,
We believe and trust in one God,
Father, Son and Holy Spirit.
Father, Son and Holy Spirit.   *adapted from* **J2**

Baptism

The vicar says to Maisie and then to Jack

Maisie / Jack, is this your faith?

Each of them answers in their own words, or

This is my faith.   **K1**

The vicar, starting with Maisie, then Jack, then Honey, pours water on each of them, saying each time

Maisie / Jack / Honey, I baptize you
in the name of the Father,
and of the Son,
and of the Holy Spirit.

The congregation respond each time

Amen.   **K2**

The vicar extends a hand towards Maisie, Jack and Honey, and says

May God, who has received you by baptism into his Church,
pour upon you the riches of his grace,
that within the company of Christ's pilgrim people
you may daily be renewed by his anointing Spirit,
and come to the inheritance of the saints in glory.
Amen.   K4

Everyone now moves back to their seats, and the vicar leads Maisie,
Jack and Honey and their godparents back to the front.

Commission

The vicar says a few words to Maisie, Jack and Honey, covering these
areas

¶ *The welcome of the Church, local and universal*

¶ *The importance of belonging to the Christian community*

¶ *The responsibilities of parents and godparents*

¶ *The challenge to grow in Christian discipleship*

¶ *The call to share God's love*

L2 *and* **L**4

The Welcome

There is one Lord, one faith, one baptism:
Maisie, Jack and Honey,
by one Spirit we are all baptized into one body.

Jill, as sponsor and godparent, says, on behalf of the congregation

We welcome you into the fellowship of faith;
we are children of the same heavenly Father;
we welcome you.

Led by the congregation leader, everyone responds

We welcome you!
We welcome you!

Everyone bursts into applause, and baptism gifts from the church to
each of the candidates are brought to them now.

based on **N**1

The Sending Out

Giving of a Lighted Candle

Jill gives candles to Maisie, Jack and one of Honey's godparents.

The vicar says

God has delivered us from the dominion of darkness
and has given us a place with the saints in light.
You have received the light of Christ;
walk in this light all the days of your life.

Led by the congregation leader, everyone responds

Shine as a light in the world,
Shine as a light in the world,
to the glory of God the Father.
to the glory of God the Father.

adapted from **R**1

Song

'Shine (from the inside out)' by Nick Jackson (Hillsong Music)

The Dismissal

*Rather than a blessing and dismissal, this part of Messy Church finishes
with Jill saying grace for the meal which is about to be enjoyed.*

Scenario 3 – St Bartholomew's

Setting the scene

St Bartholomew's (or St Bart's, as it is known locally) is a relaxed charismatic evangelical church in a market town. The church has a strong ministry among families and works closely with the local Church of England primary school. There are around 10 infant baptisms a year.

Like most baptisms at St Bart's, Latika's baptism is taking place within a Service of the Word at the 10.30 a.m. service, and the regular congregation (approximately 180) provide a warm welcome and celebratory refreshments of drinks and cake afterwards. Seats are reserved for the baptism family, and any visiting children are invited into the children's groups which meet later on in the church hall.

Before the service starts, a rolling series of notices on screen welcomes the congregation and especially those who have come to support the baptism family. This usually includes photographs (with permission) of the child who is going to be baptized.

A spoken welcome and notices are given at the start of the service and these include the encouragement for family to take photos or video of the baptism itself (but not other parts of the service) without disturbing others or blocking the view. All words for the service are projected on screens and the music is led by a band made up of drums, bass, acoustic guitar, keyboard, lead vocalist, backing vocalist and one other acoustic instrument such as flute or violin.

Notes on the service

Structure

Because the children (regulars and visitors) are invited to join the normal children's groups later in the service, the flexible structure of A Service of the Word is used. A short Liturgy of the Word focuses on the children immediately before the Liturgy of Baptism. The Bible reading and sermon for adults takes place later, after the baptism.

The children return before the end of the service, to see the Giving of a Lighted Candle and to be part of the Dismissal.

Thanksgiving Prayer for a Child

The Thanksgiving Prayer for a Child (B2) is used as an opening prayer, setting the overall background of thankfulness in which the baptism takes place.

The Decision

There is no Easter candle at St Bart's, so they have looked for other ways to use symbolism at the Decision. At the last few baptisms they have begun to use a large cross (5 feet high), which is part of the walk of witness through the town on Good Friday. At baptisms, this cross is set up beside the pulpit, and at the Decision, the candidate, parents and godparents turn to face it halfway through the questions. They remain facing the large cross for the Signing with the Cross, which follows.

Songs

Because sung worship (of mainly modern songs) is such a big part of regular worship at St Bartholomew's, songs are used wherever possible during the baptism service to express and support the mood and content of the liturgy. For instance, immediately after the Signing with the Cross, part of the song 'What a Beautiful Name' is used, which includes these words: 'What a powerful name it is... The name of Jesus Christ my King. What a powerful name it is. Nothing can stand against...'

The place of baptism

The small Victorian font which stands at the back of the church has not been used for many years. Because the worship is largely reliant on screens, the baptism itself takes place at a generously sized modern moveable font that is placed at the front of the church, but to one side rather than in the middle. When adult baptisms take place at St Bartholomew's, they use an inflatable baptism pool, but it stands in the same place as the font used for infant baptisms, as a clear signal that there is one baptism into Christ, whatever the mode and whatever the age of the candidate.

The Service

Welcome and notices

The rector welcomes everyone to the service, gives any important notices,
and a few practical announcements.

Opening prayer

During this opening Prayer of Thanksgiving, the musicians begin the
introduction to the song that follows

God our Creator,
we thank you for the wonder of new life
and for the mystery of human love.
We give thanks for all whose support and skill
surround and sustain the beginning of life.
As Jesus knew love and discipline within a human family,
may Latika grow in strength and wisdom.
As Mary knew the joys and pains of motherhood,
give Latika's parents your sustaining grace and love;
through Jesus Christ our Lord.
Amen.   **B***2*

Songs of worship

A series of songs follows, which includes 'What a Beautiful Name' by
Brooke Ligertwood and Ben Fielding.

Bible story

A short Bible story is told from one of the Gospels, using illustrations on
screen. The story is connected with the Bible reading which the adults
will hear later in the service.

One of the leaders of the children's groups follows this with a very short
simple talk.

Presentation of the Candidates

The rector gives a brief informal introduction to baptism, based on ideas found in Section **C**.

Latika is brought to the front of the church by her parents and godparents and is introduced to the congregation.

The rector says to the whole congregation

Jesus said, 'Let the children come to me. Do not stop them'.
We thank God for Latika who has come to be baptized today.
Christ loves her and welcomes her into his Church.

So I ask you all:
Will you support her as she begins her journey of faith?
We will.
Will you help her to live and grow within God's family?
We will.

The rector then says to the parents and godparents

God knows each of us by name and we are his.
Parents and godparents, you speak for Latika today.
Will you pray for her, and help her to follow Christ?
We will.   **F**4

The Decision

The rector addresses Latika through her parents and godparents

We all wander far from God and lose our way:
Christ comes to find us and welcomes us home.
In baptism we respond to his call.

Therefore I ask:
Do you turn away from sin?
I do.
Do you reject evil?
I do.

At this point, Latika, together with her parents and godparents, turns to face the large cross which stands near the pulpit.

Do you turn to Christ as Saviour?
I do.

Do you trust in him as Lord?
I do. **G***2*

The Signing with the Cross

Latika and her parents and godparents remain standing facing the large cross.

The rector makes the sign of the cross on Latika's forehead, saying

Christ claims you for his own.
Receive the sign of his cross. **H***1*

Latika's parents and godparents sign her with the cross. Those church members who help with baptism preparation are also invited to sign her.

Then the rector says

Do not be ashamed of Christ.
You are his for ever.
Stand bravely with him
against all the powers of evil,
and remain faithful to Christ to the end of your life. **H***4*

May almighty God deliver you from the powers of darkness,
and lead you in the light and obedience of Christ.
Amen. **H***5*

This is followed immediately by singing the third chorus from the song sung earlier:
'What a Beautiful Name' by Brooke Ligertwood and Ben Fielding.

While this is being sung, the baptismal party move to the font.

Prayer Over the Water

Before the prayer itself, children (and anyone else who cannot see clearly what is happening) are invited to come to the front to be near the font.

We praise you, loving Father,
for the gift of your Son Jesus.
He was baptized in the River Jordan,
where your Spirit came upon him
and revealed him as the Son you love.
He sent his followers
to baptize all who turn to him.
Now, Father, we ask you to bless this water,
that those who are baptized in it
may be cleansed in the water of life,
and, filled with your Spirit,
may know that they are loved as your children,
safe in Christ for ever.
Amen.   14

This is followed immediately by the song, 'Arms of Grace' by Beth Croft.

Profession of Faith

The rector invites everyone to profess the Christian faith

Let us affirm,
together with Latika who is being baptized,
our common faith in Jesus Christ.

Do you believe and trust in God the Father,
source of all being and life,
the one for whom we exist?
I believe and trust in him.

Do you believe and trust in God the Son,
who took our human nature,
died for us and rose again?
I believe and trust in him.

Do you believe and trust in God the Holy Spirit,
who gives life to the people of God
and makes Christ known in the world?
I believe and trust in him.

This is the faith of the Church.
This is our faith.
We believe and trust in one God,
Father, Son and Holy Spirit.   J2

Baptism

The rector baptizes Latika, saying

Latika, I baptize you in the name of the Father,
and of the Son,
and of the Holy Spirit.
Amen.   K2

The rector prays this prayer for her

May God, who has received you by baptism into his Church,
pour upon you the riches of his grace,
that within the company of Christ's pilgrim people
you may daily be renewed by his anointing Spirit,
and come to the inheritance of the saints in glory.
Amen.   K4

Commission

The brief and informal Commission by the rector includes:
¶ *The welcome of the Church, local and universal*
¶ *The importance of belonging to the Christian community*
¶ *The responsibilities of parents and godparents*
¶ *The challenge to grow in Christian discipleship*   L2

The rector concludes the Commission with the following prayer for
Latika's parents:

Faithful and loving God,
bless those who care for Latika
and grant them your gifts of love, wisdom and faith.
Pour upon them your healing and reconciling love,
and protect their home from all evil.
Fill them with the light of your presence
and establish them in the joy of your kingdom,
through Jesus Christ our Lord.
Amen.   L5

The Welcome

There is one Lord, one faith, one baptism:
Latika, by one Spirit we are all baptized into one body.
We welcome you into the fellowship of faith;
we are children of the same heavenly Father;
we welcome you.   **N**1

The congregation greet Latika with a round of applause.

During the next song, children and young people move to their groups
with their leaders.

Song

Bible Reading

Sermon

Intercessions

A member of the congregation leads a short time of intercession for:

- *The nations*
- *The renewal of the Church*
- *The oppressed*
- *The concerns of those present*

After each section the following response is used:

Your kingdom come,
your will be done.

During the prayers, background music continues quietly.

Song

During this song, children and young people return from their groups.

The Lord's Prayer

When everyone has gathered again, the rector says

Let's gather up all that we've said and sung, and all that we have prayed, as we say together the prayer that Jesus gave to all his followers.

Our Father in heaven,
hallowed be your name,
your kingdom come,
your will be done,
on earth as in heaven.
Give us today our daily bread.
Forgive us our sins
as we forgive those who sin against us.
Lead us not into temptation
but deliver us from evil.
For the kingdom, the power,
and the glory are yours
now and for ever.
Amen.

Closing notices

This includes a repeat of the invitation to stay for drinks and cake.

Blessing

The God of all grace,
who called you to his eternal glory in Christ Jesus,
establish, strengthen and settle you in the faith;
and the blessing of God almighty,
the Father, the Son, and the Holy Spirit,
be among you and remain with you always.
Amen.   Q1

Giving of a Lighted Candle

One of the older children from St Bart's gives Latika a lighted candle.

The rector says

God has delivered us from the dominion of darkness
and has given us a place with the saints in light.

You have received the light of Christ;
walk in this light all the days of your life.
**Shine as a light in the world
to the glory of God the Father.**   R*1*

The Dismissal

Go in the light and peace of Christ.
Thanks be to God.   S*1*

Final song

*The song 'We are Marching in the Light of God (Siyahamb' ekukhanyen'
kwenkhos)' (Traditional South African; translated by Anders Nyberg) is
sung as people begin to move through to the church hall for
refreshments and baptism cake.*

Scenario 4 – St John's

Setting the scene

St John's is a church set in the suburbs of a city, which thinks of itself as 'middle of the road'. A lot of the baptisms at St John's take place at the monthly all-age worship service, which they call 'All-in'. They use the flexibility of A Service of the Word as their framework, and the All-in service usually includes a mixture of songs accompanied by a guitar, and hymns accompanied by the organ.

The parish is large and includes a lot of housing, including some newly built housing estates on what used to be industrial land. This has brought more young families into the area and some of them have begun to attend the All-in service. Numbers of baptisms of infants and of older children are on the rise, though on the whole it is still possible for most baptisms to take place within a main Sunday service – mostly the All-in service, but sometimes one of the other Sunday morning services instead.

Notes to this service

The candidate

The candidate, Marcianne, is six years old, and she and her family have fairly recently moved to the area. In their previous town, they worshipped at a church in a denomination that only practised believer's baptism, and so when she was born they had a service of Infant Dedication. They have now been coming to St John's for a year, and feel that the time is right for Marcianne to be baptized. Marcianne herself has asked for this so that she can receive communion like most of the other children at the church. Though Marcianne is old enough to answer for herself, her parents and godparents will also answer with her.

The service

The Greeting and the Welcome liturgy are used at every All-in service, and they place the service within a framework of welcome and hospitality. The Collect is used without the longer Trinitarian ending, in keeping with the collects normally used at All-in services (which are generally taken from the *Common Worship* Additional Collects).

The baptism texts

At St John's there was a key PCC discussion when the Additional Baptism Texts in Accessible Language were published. They decided to use some of the alternatives (for instance, the Presentation of the Candidate, and the Signing with the Cross), but felt that the original form of the Decision in *Common Worship* (with its six-fold questions) worked well in their context.

In the case of Marcianne's baptism, because she would be answering for herself, but also having parents and godparents to answer with her, the vicar decided to use the original form of Presentation from *Common Worship*, which makes it easier to include (for the same candidate) elements for candidates able to answer for themselves and for those who have parents and godparents speaking on their behalf (see the guidance for Option 1 in Section F).

The alternative form of the Profession of Faith (J2, with its simple repeated congregational response) has been chosen because it makes it easier for those who are new to reading, or find reading harder, to join in.

Movement at the Decision

A 'river' of blue cloth is laid out at the front of the church, along the chancel step. This is used later in the service as a focus for water-drop prayers, but it is also used at the Decision. The candidate (and their parents and godparents) start in the chancel for the responses to the first three questions. Then they step across the 'river' into the main part of the church for the final three questions.

Seasonal texts

This baptism is taking place in the All-in service that falls in the season of Epiphany, and so the vicar has chosen to use some of the seasonal options for Epiphany/Baptism of Christ/Trinity, such as the Collect, the Prayer over the Water, the introduction to the Lord's Prayer, and the Blessing. Normally at St John's they choose one of the shorter simpler Prayers over the Water from the Additional Baptism Texts, as it feels more in keeping with the normal liturgical mode at All-in services.

The Service

Welcome Liturgy

The vicar gives informal welcomes and introductions and then these responses are used

Young and old,
we welcome you!
Happy and sad,
we welcome you!
Regular and visitor,
we welcome you!
Quiet and noisy,
we welcome you!
All God's people,
we welcome you!

Song

'Everybody's Welcome', by Nigel Hemming – a simple song of gathering and welcome.

Presentation of the Candidate

The vicar gives an informal introduction to baptism, based on the ideas in the seasonal Introduction to Baptism C3.

The vicar then says

Marcianne, do you wish to be baptized?

She replies in her own words, or simply

I do.   F1

The vicar addresses the whole congregation

Faith is the gift of God to his people.
In baptism the Lord is adding to our number
    those whom he is calling.
People of God, will you welcome Marcianne
and uphold her in her new life in Christ?
With the help of God, we will.   F2

The vicar then says to Marcianne's parents and godparents

Parents and godparents, the Church receives Marcianne with joy.
Today we are trusting God for her growth in faith.
Will you pray for her, draw her by your example into the community
of faith and walk with her in the way of Christ?
With the help of God, we will.

In baptism Marcianne begins her journey in faith.
You speak for her today.
Will you care for her, and help her to take her place
within the life and worship of Christ's Church?
With the help of God, we will.   **F**3

Collect

Lord of all time and eternity,
you opened heaven's gate and revealed yourself as Father
by the voice that called Jesus your beloved Son,
baptizing him, in the power of the Spirit:
reveal yourself to us now, to claim us as your children,
and so complete the heavenly work of our rebirth
in the waters of the new creation;
through Jesus Christ your Son our Lord.
Amen.   *adapted from* **D**2

Bible Reading

The Bible reading is retold using illustrations from a children's Bible

Song

Craft activity

*Congregation members are invited go to one of four points round the
church building and do the simple craft activity there – each activity is
related to the Bible reading.*

Talk

This draws on the Bible reading and also includes an outline of what baptism means and its implications, drawing on the themes outlined in the Commissions L2 (for those unable to answer for themselves) and L4 (for those able to answer for themselves).

Hymn

The Decision

Marcianne and her parents and godparents come to the front of the church and stand in the chancel, on the far side of the 'river' of blue cloth.

In baptism, God calls us out of darkness into his marvellous light.
To follow Christ means dying to sin and rising to new life with him.

Therefore I ask:

Do you reject the devil and all rebellion against God?
I reject them.

Do you renounce the deceit and corruption of evil?
I renounce them.

Do you repent of the sins that separate us from God and neighbour?
I repent of them.

Marcianne and her parents and godparents step across the 'river' into the main part of the church.

Do you turn to Christ as Saviour?
I turn to Christ.

Do you submit to Christ as Lord?
I submit to Christ.

Do you come to Christ, the way, the truth and the life?
I come to Christ.   **G**1

Signing with the Cross

The vicar uses oil to make the sign of the cross on Marcianne's forehead, saying

Christ claims you for his own.
Receive the sign of his cross.   **H**1

The vicar invites Marcianne's parents and godparents to sign her with
the cross, and then says

Do not be ashamed of Christ.
You are his for ever.
Stand bravely with him
against all the powers of evil,
and remain faithful to Christ to the end of your life. H4

May almighty God deliver you from the powers of darkness,
and lead you in the light and obedience of Christ.
Amen. H5

The vicar leads Marcianne, her parents, and her godparents to gather
at the font at the back of the church, and invites the congregation to
turn to face it.

Prayer over the Water

The vicar says

Father, for your gift of water in creation,
we give you thanks and praise.

For your Spirit, sweeping over the waters, bringing light and life,
we give you thanks and praise.

For your Son Jesus Christ our Lord, baptized in the river Jordan,
we give you thanks and praise.

For your new creation, brought to birth by water and the Spirit,
we give you thanks and praise.

For your grace bestowed upon us your children,
washing away our sins,
we give you thanks and praise.

Father, accept our sacrifice of praise;
may your holy and life-giving Spirit move upon these waters.
Lord, receive our prayer.

Restore through them the beauty of your creation,
and bring those who are baptized
to new birth in the family of your Church.
Lord, receive our prayer.

Drown sin in the waters of judgement,
anoint your children with power from on high,
and make them one with Christ in the freedom of your kingdom.
Lord, receive our prayer.

For all might, majesty, dominion and power are yours,
now and for ever.
Alleluia. Amen.   17

Profession of Faith

The vicar invites everyone to profess the Christian faith

Let us affirm,
together with Marcianne who is being baptized,
our common faith in Jesus Christ.

Do you believe and trust in God the Father,
source of all being and life,
the one for whom we exist?
I believe and trust in him.

Do you believe and trust in God the Son,
who took our human nature,
died for us and rose again?
I believe and trust in him.

Do you believe and trust in God the Holy Spirit,
who gives life to the people of God
and makes Christ known in the world?
I believe and trust in him.

This is the faith of the Church.
This is our faith.
We believe and trust in one God,
Father, Son and Holy Spirit.   J2

Baptism

The minister says

Marcianne, is this your faith?

Marcianne answers in her own words, or

This is my faith.   **K**1

The vicar baptizes Marcianne, saying

Marcianne Rebecca, I baptize you in the name of the Father,
and of the Son,
and of the Holy Spirit.
Amen.   **K**2

The vicar prays for Marcianne, saying

May God, who has received you by baptism into his Church,
pour upon you the riches of his grace,
that within the company of Christ's pilgrim people
you may daily be renewed by his anointing Spirit,
and come to the inheritance of the saints in glory.
Amen.   **K**4

Address to the Newly Baptized

Marcianne, today God has touched you with his love
and given you a place among his people.
God promises to be with you
in joy and in sorrow, to be your guide in life,
and to bring you safely to heaven.
In baptism God invites you on a life-long journey.
Together with God's people
you must explore the way of Jesus
and grow in friendship with God, in love for his people,
and in serving others.
With us you will listen to the word of God
and receive the gifts of God.   **L**7

The vicar continues

And so we gladly welcome you.

The Welcome

There is one Lord, one faith, one baptism:
Marcianne, by one Spirit we are all baptized into one body.
We welcome you into the fellowship of faith;
we are children of the same heavenly Father;
we welcome you.   **N**1

Marcianne is greeted with applause.
The vicar gives her baptism certificate to her.

The Peace

If anyone is in Christ, there is a new creation.
The old has passed away; the new has come.   **N**4

The peace of the Lord be always with you
and also with you.

Let us offer one another a sign of peace.

All may exchange a sign of peace.   **N**3

Hymn

During this hymn the offering is taken and Marcianne, her parents,
and her godparents return to their seats.

Offering prayer

As we gather as God's community,
welcoming its newest member,
we respond to all that God has given us.
We make our lives an offering,
our time, our money and our love.

A moment of silence is kept.

Generous God,
in the waters of baptism you pour your love upon us
and call us to work with you in your world.
We offer this money as a token of all we are and have:
use it and use us, in the service of your world,
and to the glory of your name.
Amen.

Water drop prayers

Pieces of paper in the shape of water drops are handed out, along with pens and pencils. Everyone is invited to write or draw on their water drop a prayer or the first name of someone they want to pray for.

While music plays in the background, they are invited to bring their water drops to the front of the church and place them on the 'river' of blue cloth laid out there.

The Lord's Prayer

In baptism God declares that we are his children, whom he loves;
so let us pray **M**3a

Our Father, who art in heaven,
hallowed be thy name;
thy kingdom come;
thy will be done;
on earth as it is in heaven.
Give us this day our daily bread.
And forgive us our trespasses,
as we forgive those who trespass against us.
And lead us not into temptation;
but deliver us from evil.
For thine is the kingdom,
the power and the glory,
for ever and ever.
Amen.

Notices

Song

During the final song, the vicar leads Marcianne and her close family and godparents to the back of the church where they gather at the font again.

Blessing

God, who in his Christ gives us a spring of water
welling up to eternal life,
perfect in you the image of his glory;
and the blessing of God almighty,
the Father, the Son, and the Holy Spirit,
be among you and remain with you always.
Amen.   **Q***2*

Giving of a Lighted Candle

God has delivered us from the dominion of darkness
and has given us a place with the saints in light.

A lighted candle is given to Marcianne.

Marcianne, you have received the light of Christ;
walk in this light all the days of your life.
**Shine as a light in the world
to the glory of God the Father.**   **R***1*

Dismissal

We go in the light of Christ.
We go in the light of Christ.

We go in the peace of Christ.
We go in the peace of Christ.

Thanks be to God.
Thanks be to God.   *adapted from* **S***1*

Scenario 5 – St Mary's

Setting the scene

St Mary's is a church in a liberal Catholic tradition with a large nineteenth-century building located in the suburbs of a city. Cassius and Serena (babies from two different families) are being baptized at the monthly Sunday afternoon baptism service.

The housing close to the church is mainly Victorian terraces and some Edwardian semis, an area built for industrial workers but now with substantial areas of gentrification. Further afield in the parish is an extensive estate of social housing. There is a church school which was rebuilt on a new site in the 1960s, and the old building has been adapted to create a community centre that is widely used by people in the neighbourhood. Part of it houses a day nursery and pre-school: two church members are on its management committee.

For the last five years the church has employed a part-time young families worker, who has worked hard to liaise with the local community through the school, the nursery and the community centre. The number of baptisms has grown during this time and baptism families often bring a large number of friends and neighbours, including significant numbers of young children.

It is often difficult for these people to arrange to attend the main 9.30 a.m. Parish Eucharist and so the PCC decided to experiment with offering a monthly baptism service on Sunday afternoons. A significant number of the regular congregation have committed to attending the service, so there is always a lay presence to welcome people and support the clergy and the families worker, and to help with the leading of worship. In particular, a musician is always present, together with someone who can set up and manage the IT and audio systems.

Families are always invited to attend a Parish Eucharist at some point in the month following the baptism. If they are able to attend, they bring the newly baptized child(ren) forward before the Peace: the congregation repeat their pledge of support (from the Presentation – the first part of F4, suitably adjusted to reflect the fact that the baptism has already taken place) and the Welcome is repeated (N1). The family is given the baptism certificate and cards for the godparents. If the family are not able to attend a Parish Eucharist, the certificate and godparent cards are delivered by hand to the family's home, along with information about forthcoming special services or activities for children and families.

Notes on the service

The candidates

Serena is brought for baptism by her mum, and is supported by three godparents. Cassius has been brought by his parents, and has four godparents. The baptismal party is therefore a significant number of people, so it is important to make sure that there is plenty of space for them all at the front and around the font.

The worship leaders and supporters

The service is usually conducted by two ministers: a priest (either the vicar, or one of the two self-supporting assistant clergy) and a lay person who acts as a kind of animateur/cantor/deacon to lead the congregation in the responses. Others are present to welcome the congregation and ensure that people are at ease and can be helped as and when necessary.

Using simple signs

People unused to participating in worship are often confused and embarrassed when they are required to make responses and answer questions in a public context. This can be exacerbated where people have difficulty reading quickly or when they might be trying to care for young children, especially if they are holding them in their arms, so that it is difficult to hold a service sheet or card.

A member of the congregation who is a school teacher suggested that one way to address this, and to draw on the predominantly kinaesthetic preferences of a significant proportion of people, might be to use very simple signs to cue and accompany some of the verbal responses required of parents and godparents, and indeed, the whole congregation. The worship sub-committee therefore decided to experiment with using Makaton signs. These were developed primarily to help interaction by children and adults who experience communication difficulties, but are now used widely in early years settings. The action of making the signs supports and empowers the verbal response or may, in some cases, replace it.

The sign used in the context of this service is the 'thumbs up' sign. A further, simple development of this is the 'Amen' sign.

The 'Amen' sign requires the 'thumbs up' sign with both hands; the hands are held apart at waist height and shoulder width at the beginning of the word and then drawn together to meet in front of the body.

Just before a response is to be spoken, the animateur raises his or her hand and then forms the 'thumbs up' sign to cue the response. The congregation respond with the sign as they say the words, led by the animateur.

Points at which the signs might be used during the service are indicated as follows:

'Thumbs up'   <

Amen   > <

Using the building

Along with the use of the simple signs, the worship sub-committee also decided to try to use the large building more actively by incorporating more movement into baptism services. Different parts of the building are used for each stage of the service, giving a sense of movement and journey as the service unfolds.

Using images

At the Prayer over the Water, three large printed images are used (mounted on card so that they can be held up):

- an image of the sea or a large body of water;

- an image of Christ;

- an image to suggest the Spirit – a dove or a flame.

Gospel readings

At the Sunday afternoon baptisms, one of two standard Gospel readings are generally used: Mark 1.1-11 (the baptism of Jesus); or Mark 10.13-16 (Jesus blesses the children). Children (and their parents) are invited to come and sit at the front, around the Gospel reader, who takes on the role of a storyteller, perhaps sitting in a special chair.

A Godly Play approach is taken. Listeners bring to the storyteller baskets prepared with materials to help the storytelling. The storyteller learns the story by heart from a biblical text, not a retelling.

The story is followed by a reflection using the four Godly Play questions outlined in the service below.

Hymns and songs

With members of the regular congregation there to give a lead, they try to include some singing in every baptism, focusing on simple songs that are either well known or easily learnt.

'I am the church' by Donald Avery and Richard Marsh is a simple description of the Church with easy actions, which they often use as a focus at the Commission. It can be found in *Junior Praise 2* and *Complete Junior Praise, Hymns of Glory, Songs of Praise* and *Big Blue Planet*.

'This little light of mine' makes a simple but engaging song for the Dismissal. It is traditional and well known, and is found in very many books in a variety of forms.

The Peruvian Gloria (now in many hymnbooks), or another simple call and response piece is sometimes used to facilitate singing among those unfamiliar with church texts.

Play materials

The Mother's Union at St Mary's have taken it upon themselves to provide some simple and relevant play materials for young children at every baptism service. These pick up on baptismal and watery themes, and are available in one of the side aisles. One of the MU members is always at the service to set these up, to act as host for children and their parents who come to use them, and to tidy them up at the end.

Leading the congregation and putting them at ease

The animateur is always introduced at the start, and rehearses a few responses with the congregation, and the sign that accompanies them, making sure that people know how to watch for cues.

The musician often gets the congregation to practise one of the simple songs being used in the service immediately before the service, which serves to gather the congregation and get them used to participating.

The Service

Preparation

The whole congregation are seated, facing the front of the church. Cassius and Serena, with their parents and godparents, are seated at the front of the congregation.

The two ministers stand together and face the congregation.

Greeting

The priest says

Welcome in the name of Christ.
God's grace, mercy and peace be with you
and also with you.

from New Patterns for Worship, *Section A, Greeting A2*

Words of welcome or introduction may be said. The animateur is introduced and explains how the signs will be used.

Introduction to Baptism

A large jug of water is brought to the front and placed on a table by a member of the church.

The priest says these, or similar words

Today we welcome Serena and Cassius as they come to be baptized.
In baptism, God calls us to be his friends.
He travels beside us on a journey of faith
    that we make with all Christian people across the world,
seeking the coming of God's eternal kingdom
    of forgiveness, love and peace.

Adapted from material in Section **C**

The Collect Prayer

The priest introduces a short silence, inviting everyone to pray in their
own hearts for Cassius and Serena, and then says

Heavenly Father,
by the power of your Holy Spirit
you give your faithful people new life in the water of baptism.
Guide and strengthen us by the same Spirit,
that we who are born again may serve you in faith and love,
and grow into the full stature of your Son, Jesus Christ,
who is alive and reigns with you
in the unity of the Holy Spirit
now and for ever.

Amen. > <   **D**1

The Liturgy of the Word

Gospel Reading

Mark 1.1-11

The reader sits in a large 'storyteller's chair' and children and others in the congregation are invited to come and sit around him or her.

The story basket is brought forward by one of the children and the reader uses it to tell the story.

Response

The reader then invites everyone to ponder these questions, inviting responses from children or adults

I wonder what you liked best about this story?

I wonder what was most important about this story?

I wonder where you are in the story, or if any part of the story is about you?

I wonder if there is any part of the story we could leave out and have all the story we need?

If people moved to sit close to the Gospel reader, they now move back to their seats.

Song

As they move, everyone sings 'Out of the flowing river' by Leith Fisher (found in 'Hymns of Glory, Songs of Praise', or can be downloaded from the Wild Goose Publications website: www.ionabooks.com)

The Liturgy of Baptism

Presentation of the Candidates

Serena and Cassius are brought by their parents and godparents to stand beside the ministers at the front of the church. They face the congregation.

The priest addresses the whole congregation

Jesus said, 'Let the children come to me. Do not stop them'.
We thank God for Serena and Cassius who have come to be baptized today.
Christ loves them and welcomes them into his Church.

So I ask you all:

Will you support these children as they begin their journey
of faith?
We will. <
Will you help them to live and grow within God's family?
We will. <

The priest then addresses the parents and godparents

God knows each of us by name and we are his.
Parents and godparents, you speak for Serena and Cassius today.
Will you pray for them, and help them to follow Christ?
We will.   **F4**

The priest invites the whole congregation to face the font.

An older child from one of the families is invited to light a large candle standing at the east side of the font.

Another child from one of the families is then invited to carry the large jug of water (that was brought forward earlier) to the font.

The ministers together with the parents and godparents and the candidates, walk towards the font, following the person carrying the jug of water. They stop when they get near the font, and remain facing it.

The jug is placed close to the font, somewhere it can be seen.

The Decision

The priest says to the parents and godparents

We all wander far from God and lose our way:
Christ comes to find us and welcomes us home.
In baptism we respond to his call.

Therefore I ask:
Do you turn away from sin?
I do.
Do you reject evil?
I do.

The parents, godparents and the candidates are led around the font so that they now stand behind the font and face the candle from the other direction.

Do you turn to Christ as Saviour?
I do.
Do you trust in him as Lord?
I do.   **G**2

Signing with the Cross

The priest makes the sign of the cross on the forehead of each candidate, saying

Christ claims you for his own.
Receive the sign of his cross.   **H**1

The priest may invite parents and godparents to sign Cassius and Serena with the cross.

When they have been signed, the priest says

Do not be ashamed of Christ.
You are his for ever.
Stand bravely with him
against all the powers of evil,
and remain faithful to Christ to the end of your life.   **H**4

May almighty God deliver you from the powers of darkness,
and lead you in the light and obedience of Christ.
Amen. > <   **H**5

Prayer over the Water

The whole congregation are invited to gather around the families at the font. Children and others who cannot easily see are invited to come close to the font. The priest invites one of the older children present to pour the water from the large jug into the font.

Three images accompany this prayer: (1) an image of the sea or a large body of water; (2) an image of Christ, and (3) an image to suggest the Spirit. Members of the baptism party are invited to hold up each image when the animateur indicates to them.

The priest stands before the water of baptism and says

Praise God who made heaven and earth,
who keeps his promise for ever.

Let us give thanks to the Lord our God.
It is right to give thanks and praise.   I1

[Image 1]

Loving Father, we thank you for your servant Moses,
who led your people through the waters of the Red Sea
to freedom in the Promised Land.

[Image 2]

We thank you for your Son Jesus,
who has passed through the deep waters of death
and opened for all the way of salvation.

[Image 3]

Now send your Spirit,
that those who are washed in this water
may die with Christ and rise with him,
to find true freedom as your children,
alive in Christ for ever.
Amen. > <   I3

Profession of Faith

The priest says

Let us affirm, together with Serena and Cassius
who are being baptized,
our common faith in Jesus Christ.

Do you believe and trust in God the Father,
source of all being and life,
the one for whom we exist?
I believe and trust in him. <

Do you believe and trust in God the Son,
who took our human nature,
died for us and rose again?
I believe and trust in him. <

Do you believe and trust in God the Holy Spirit,
who gives life to the people of God
and makes Christ known in the world?
I believe and trust in him. <

This is the faith of the Church.
This is our faith.
We believe and trust in one God,
Father, Son and Holy Spirit. < < <   *J*2

Baptism

The priest baptizes Serena *and* Cassius, *saying each time*

Serena Louise Annette / Cassius Francis,
I baptize you in the name of the Father,
and of the Son,
and of the Holy Spirit.
Amen. > <   *K*2

The priest prays this prayer over each of them after they have been baptized.

May God, who has received you by baptism into his Church,
pour upon you the riches of his grace,
that within the company of Christ's pilgrim people
you may daily be renewed by his anointing Spirit,
and come to the inheritance of the saints in glory.
Amen. > <   *K*4

Giving of a Lighted Candle

The animateur lights a candle for each child from the large candle
beside the font used at the Decision. Each of the newly baptized, or one
of their godparents, is given the candle.

Then the priest says

God has delivered us from the dominion of darkness
and has given us a place with the saints in light.

You have received the light of Christ;
walk in this light all the days of your life.
Shine as a light in the world
to the glory of God the Father. <   K5

Song

The animateur leads the singing of the song 'I am the Church' by
Donald Avery and Richard Marsh. The verses are sung by the animateur
and members of the regular church congregation, with everyone joining
in and singing the refrain.

During the song, the ministers and the families of Serena and Cassius
walk in procession with the candles to the front of the church. The
congregation follow on, back to their seats.

Commission

The priest briefly addresses the congregation, parents and godparents
using the song they have just sung to note the welcome of the Church,
local and universal, the support and role of the Christian community,
the role of parents and godparents and the assurance of God's blessing.

Address to the Newly Baptized

Serena and Cassius,
today God has touched you with his love
and given you a place among his people.
God promises to be with you
in joy and in sorrow, to be your guide in life,
and to bring you safely to heaven.
In baptism God invites you on a life-long journey.
Together with all God's people
you must explore the way of Jesus
and grow in friendship with God, in love for his people,
and in serving others.
With us you will listen to the word of God
and receive the gifts of God. **L**7

Each child is given a small Bible story book as the last sentence is said.

*The candles are now extinguished and the ministers, together with the
people carrying the newly baptized move into the centre of the church.
The congregation turn to face them.*

The Welcome and Peace

There is one Lord, one faith, one baptism:
Serena and Cassius, by one Spirit we are all baptized into one body.
We welcome you into the fellowship of faith;
we are children of the same heavenly Father;
we welcome you. **N**1

The congregation greet Serena and Cassius with applause.

We are all one in Christ Jesus.
We belong to him through faith,
heirs of the promise of the Spirit of peace. **N**2

The peace of the Lord be always with you
and also with you. < **N**3

*The animateur may suggest that peace is exchanged in appropriate ways –
a handshake, a high-five or some other suitable sign.*

After exchanging the Peace, all return to their places, facing the front.

Prayers of Intercession

The prayers are led by the priest (and others indicated below) and include the following:

A prayer for parents/guardians

Faithful and loving God,
bless those who care for these children
and grant them your gifts of love, wisdom and faith.
Pour upon them your healing and reconciling love,
and protect their home from all evil.
Fill them with the light of your presence
and establish them in the joy of your kingdom,
through Jesus Christ our Lord.
Amen. > <   **L**5

A prayer led by Serena's brother

Thank you, God, for my new sister, Serena.
Help me play my part in loving her and caring for her.
Make us good friends
so that we can laugh when life is happy
and help each other when things are hard.
In the name of Jesus, our Saviour and our friend.
Amen. > <

A prayer led by Cassius's grandma

God, our creator,
thank you for this new addition to our family.
Help us to know how to encourage our children
as they care for their family,
rejoicing at steps forward
and supporting when there are setbacks.
Sustain us all, now and in the years to come.
Amen. > <

The prayers conclude with this prayer, led by the priest.

Loving God,
as we celebrate together the baptism of Serena and Cassius
and recognize the blessings of family and friends,
we pray for those near and far
for whom today has been a lonely day,
for those who are struggling to feed their children,
for those whose lives are dominated by war and fear.
Bring your kingdom nearer
in their lives as well as ours.
We ask it in the name of Jesus.
Amen. > <

The Lord's Prayer

As your children, born again in Christ, we say   **M***1a*
Our Father, who art in heaven,
hallowed be thy name;
thy kingdom come;
thy will be done;
on earth as it is in heaven.
Give us this day our daily bread.
And forgive us our trespasses,
as we forgive those who trespass against us.
And lead us not into temptation;
but deliver us from evil.
For thine is the kingdom,
the power and the glory,
for ever and ever.
Amen. > <

The Sending Out

The Blessing

The God of all grace,
who called you to his eternal glory in Christ Jesus,
establish, strengthen and settle you in the faith;
and the blessing of God almighty,
the Father, the Son, and the Holy Spirit,
be among you and remain with you always.
Amen. > <   Q1

The Dismissal

The candles of the newly baptized are lit again.

Go in the light and peace of Christ.
Thanks be to God. <   S1

The ministers and the families of Serena and Cassius walk to the church door with the lighted candles while everybody sings 'This little light of mine'.

At the door the candles are put out and the families and the ministers greet the congregation as they leave.

Scenario 6 – St Helen's

Setting the scene

St Helen's is an urban parish church, built in the nineteenth century. It has a long-standing Catholic tradition, and the Sunday Parish Mass is the centre of its life.

The regular congregation number around 80. There is a choir, which leads the singing of a musical setting of the Eucharist, and a team of altar servers which includes a number of older children and young people – many of whom come from the local church school. Young children have their own teaching in the adjacent parish room (leaving the congregation during the Gloria and normally returning during the Peace, though for a baptism they rejoin the congregation earlier). The congregation value a sense of beauty, dignity and wonder in worship, with all the senses engaged, and there is a warmth of atmosphere and welcome and a strong sense of community life.

Baptisms take place during the Parish Mass, and, after an initial meeting with the parish priest, a team of parishioners visit the parents of infants being baptized to explain what happens at the service, and to lead them through some preparation. As the families arrive for the service itself, this team makes them welcome and sits with them towards the front of the church. After the service they bring them to share the refreshments that are being served at the back of the church, and they also make a follow-up visit on the anniversary of the baptism, taking a greeting card from the church.

The parish does not hold baptisms in the seasons of Advent and Lent, and the service described here takes place during Eastertide. The Paschal candle, decorated with flowers, is standing in a place of honour at the front of the church, and the musicians have chosen joyful hymns and anthems, taking account, too, of the fact that many in the congregation will not be regular churchgoers.

Notes on the service

Candidate

In this service, Joel, a seven-month-old baby, is being baptized.

Presentation of the Candidate

The Presentation takes place towards the beginning of the service, as the presiding priest introduces the celebration and welcomes the congregation. The parents and godparents are invited forward to the chancel step, where the children have also gathered before they proceed to their activities.

The Collect and Readings

The Collect and Readings are those set for this Sunday in Eastertide. On this occasion the presiding priest has chosen for there to be only one reading before the Gospel, and this will be from the Acts of the Apostles in order to continue the Eastertide reading from that book (as indicated in the Lectionary). While the congregation are used to an acclamation preceding the Gospel reading, here the director of music has chosen a well-known Easter hymn which uses 'Alleluia' as a refrain.

Place of baptism

The font is at the back of the church, near the entrance. During the procession to the font the organist usually gently improvises while everyone moves, but for this baptism in Eastertide the parish deacon leads the congregation in words from A Litany of the Resurrection.

Prayer over the Water

In Eastertide the responsive seasonal prayer over the water is used (item I8). A cantor sings the first part of the response ('Saving God') and the congregation join in with 'give us life'. The musical chant is very simple, and the congregation know it well and give a good lead.

Eucharistic Prayer

Eucharistic Prayer E is normally used at St Helen's when there is a baptism. This is a relatively short eucharistic prayer, but with the opportunity to use an extended preface to maximize the relevant seasonal flavour of the service.

Giving of a Lighted Candle

Generally at St Helen's the presiding priest prefers the Giving of the Lighted Candle to take place after the Clothing, but since a Paschal candle is at the front of the church during Eastertide (rather than standing next to the font as usual), for ease of liturgical flow, this comes at the end of this service.

The Service

Preparation

Gathering hymn

As this hymn is sung, the choir and ministers process into the church, led by the servers with incense, lights and cross.

The president says

In the name of the Father,
and of the Son,
and of the Holy Spirit.
Amen.

The Greeting

The Lord be with you
and also with you.
Alleluia. Christ is risen.
He is risen indeed. Alleluia.

The president gives an informal welcome, introducing the theme of the liturgy, based on item C4.

The parents and godparents are invited to the front of the church and introduced to the congregation.

Presentation of the Candidate

The president addresses the whole congregation

Faith is the gift of God to his people.
In baptism the Lord is adding to our number
    those whom he is calling.
People of God, will you welcome Joel
and uphold him in his new life in Christ?
With the help of God, we will.   F2

The president then says to the parents and godparents

Parents and godparents, the Church receives Joel with joy.
Today we are trusting God for his growth in faith.
Will you pray for him, draw him by your example into the community
of faith and walk with him in the way of Christ?
With the help of God, we will.

In baptism Joel begins his journey in faith.
You speak for him today.
Will you care for him, and help him to take his place within the life
and worship of Christ's Church?
With the help of God, we will.   **F**3

Gloria in Excelsis

*The choir lead the congregation in the singing of the Gloria as the
parents and godparents return to their places.*

Young children go out to the parish room for their activities.

Collect

The president introduces a period of silent prayer with the words

Let us pray

and then sings the Collect of the Day, to which the people respond

Amen.

The Liturgy of the Word

First Reading

The reading from the Acts of the Apostles is used.

At the end the reader says

This is the word of the Lord.
Thanks be to God. $\qquad$ E*1*

Hymn

'The strife is o'er, the battle done' (C17th Latin hymn, translated by Francis Pott, 1861)

Gospel Reading

When the Gospel is announced the deacon says

The Lord be with you
and also with you.
Hear the Gospel of our Lord Jesus Christ according to *N.*
Glory to you, O Lord.

At the end

This is the Gospel of the Lord.
Praise to you, O Christ. $\qquad$ E*2*

Sermon

In the course of the sermon the preacher includes the themes of the Commission:

¶ *The welcome of the Church, local and universal*
¶ *The importance of belonging to the Christian community*
¶ *The responsibilities of parents and godparents*
¶ *The challenge to grow in Christian discipleship* $\qquad$ L*2*

The Liturgy of Baptism

The Decision

The president invites the parents and godparents to bring Joel to the front of the church where the Paschal candle is standing.

The president addresses Joel through his parents and godparents

In baptism, God calls us out of darkness into his marvellous light.
To follow Christ means dying to sin and rising to new life with him.

Therefore I ask:

Do you reject the devil and all rebellion against God?
I reject them.
Do you renounce the deceit and corruption of evil?
I renounce them.
Do you repent of the sins that separate us from God and neighbour?
I repent of them.

Do you turn to Christ as Saviour?
I turn to Christ.
Do you submit to Christ as Lord?
I submit to Christ.
Do you come to Christ, the way, the truth and the life?
I come to Christ.   **G**1

The Signing with the Cross

The president makes the sign of the cross on Joel's forehead with the Oil of Baptism, saying

Christ claims you for his own.
Receive the sign of his cross.   H1

The parents and godparents also trace the sign of the cross on Joel's forehead, after which the president says

Do not be ashamed to confess the faith of Christ crucified.
Fight valiantly as a disciple of Christ
against sin, the world and the devil,
and remain faithful to Christ to the end of your life.   H2

May almighty God deliver you from the powers of darkness,
restore in you the image of his glory,
and lead you in the light and obedience of Christ.
Amen.   H3

Procession to the Font

The servers with cross and lights lead a procession to the font.

Joel, with his parents, godparents and family, follows the presiding priest. The rest of the congregation follow on and gather around the font – including the children who have returned from their activities in the parish room.

While this procession takes place, the deacon leads the congregation in words from A Litany of the Resurrection.

A Litany of the Resurrection

O give thanks to the Lord, for he is gracious:
and his mercy endures for ever.

He has loved us from all eternity:
for his mercy endures for ever.

And remembered us when we were in trouble:
for his mercy endures for ever.

For us and for our salvation he came down from heaven:
for his mercy endures for ever.

He became incarnate of the Holy Spirit and the Virgin Mary
and was made man:
for his mercy endures for ever.

By his cross and passion he has redeemed the world:
for his mercy endures for ever.

And has washed us from our sins in his own blood:
for his mercy endures for ever.

On the third day he rose again:
for his mercy endures for ever.

And has given us the victory:
for his mercy endures for ever.

He ascended into heaven:
for his mercy endures for ever.

And opened wide for us the everlasting doors:
for his mercy endures for ever.

He is seated at the right hand of the Father:
for his mercy endures for ever.

And ever lives to make intercession for us:
for his mercy endures for ever.

**Glory to the Father and to the Son
and to the Holy Spirit;
as it was in the beginning is now
and shall be for ever.
Amen.** **T**4

Prayer over the Water

The president stands before the water of baptism and says

Praise God who made heaven and earth,
who keeps his promise for ever.

Let us give thanks to the Lord our God.
It is right to give thanks and praise.   ¹7

*This prayer follows. Responses in italic are sung by a cantor; everyone
joins in singing the response in bold.*

Almighty God, whose Son Jesus Christ
was baptized in the river Jordan,
we thank you for the gift of water
to cleanse us and revive us.
Saving God,
give us life.

We thank you that through the waters of the Red Sea
you led your people out of slavery
to freedom in the Promised Land.
Saving God,
give us life.

We thank you that through the deep waters of death
        you brought your Son,
and raised him to life in triumph.
Saving God,
give us life.

Bless this water, that your servants who are washed in it
may be made one with Christ in his death and in his resurrection,
to be cleansed and delivered from all sin.
Saving God,
give us life.

Send your Holy Spirit upon them,
bring them to new birth in the household of faith
and raise them with Christ to full and eternal life;
for all might, majesty, authority and power are yours,
now and for ever. Amen.
Saving God,
give us life.   ¹8

Profession of Faith

The president addresses the congregation

Brothers and sisters, I ask you to profess
together with Joel
the faith of the Church.

Do you believe and trust in God the Father?
I believe in God, the Father almighty,
creator of heaven and earth.

Do you believe and trust in his Son Jesus Christ?
I believe in Jesus Christ, his only Son, our Lord,
who was conceived by the Holy Spirit,
born of the Virgin Mary, suffered under Pontius Pilate,
was crucified, died, and was buried;
he descended to the dead.
On the third day he rose again;
he ascended into heaven,
he is seated at the right hand of the Father,
and he will come to judge the living and the dead.

Do you believe and trust in the Holy Spirit?
I believe in the Holy Spirit,
the holy catholic Church,
the communion of saints,
the forgiveness of sins,
the resurrection of the body,
and the life everlasting.
Amen.   **J***1*

Baptism

The president pours water on Joel three times, saying

Joel Arthur, I baptize you in the name of the Father,
and of the Son,
and of the Holy Spirit.
Amen.   **K***2*

Joel is wrapped with a white shawl as the president says

Joel, you have been clothed with Christ.
As many as are baptized into Christ have put on Christ.   **K***3*

The president anoints the crown of Joel's head with the oil of chrism,
making the sign of the chi-rho (the first two letters of the Greek word for
Christ), signifying Christos, the Anointed One.

The anointing is accompanied by this prayer.

May God, who has received you by baptism into his Church,
pour upon you the riches of his grace,
that within the company of Christ's pilgrim people
you may daily be renewed by his anointing Spirit,
and come to the inheritance of the saints in glory.
Amen.   K4

The Welcome

There is one Lord, one faith, one baptism:
Joel, by one Spirit we are all baptized into one body.
We welcome you into the fellowship of faith;
we are children of the same heavenly Father;
we welcome you.   N1

The congregation greet Joel with applause.

The president sprinkles the congregation as they recall their own
baptism, and the procession returns everyone to their places.

While this is taking place the choir lead everyone in singing some verses
from the hymn 'All creatures of our God and King'.

> Thou flowing water, pure and clear,
> make music for thy Lord to hear,
>   Alleluia, alleluia!
> Thou fire so masterful and bright,
> that givest us both warmth and light:
>   O praise him, O praise him,
>   Alleluia, alleluia, alleluia!
>
> Let all things their Creator bless,
> and worship him in humbleness,
>   O praise him! Alleluia!
> Praise, praise the Father, praise the Son,
> and praise the Spirit, Three in One:
>   O praise him, O praise him,
>   Alleluia, alleluia, alleluia!

Words: St Francis of Assisi 1182–1226
Tr. William Draper 1855–1933

Prayers of Intercession

A member of the congregation leads the prayers

Father, we thank you that by baptism
you have raised Joel with Christ
to new life in the Spirit.
Guide and protect him with your grace,
that he may follow you all his days
and grow in knowledge and love of you.

Father, by the victory of your Son,
give light to the world.

May Christ who conquered sin and death
keep his whole Church faithful to his gospel.
Help us always to hold fast to truth
and to walk in the way of life.

Father, by the victory of your Son,
give light to the world.

May the Holy Spirit fill the hearts and minds of all nations
to unite the world in peace and love.
By your healing power restore all that is broken
and unite us with you, our God and Father.

Father, by the victory of your Son,
give light to the world.   **M**4

The Liturgy of the Eucharist

The Peace

The president introduces the Peace.

The risen Christ came and stood among his disciples
    and said 'Peace be with you'.
Then were they glad when they saw the Lord. Alleluia.   **N5**

The peace of the Lord be always with you
and also with you.

The deacon says

Let us offer one another a sign of peace.

All may exchange a sign of peace.   **N3**

Hymn

*During this hymn the altar is prepared and the offerings of the people
are gathered.*

Preparation of the Table

Taking of the Bread and Wine

Creator of all,
you wash away our sins,
you give us new birth by the Spirit,
and redeem us in the blood of Christ.
As we celebrate the resurrection,
renew your gift of life within us.
We ask this in the name of Jesus Christ the risen Lord.
Amen.

The Eucharistic Prayer

The president sings

The Lord be with you
and also with you.

Lift up your hearts.
We lift them to the Lord.

Let us give thanks to the Lord our God.
It is right to give thanks and praise.

It is indeed right, our duty and our joy,
always and everywhere to give you thanks,
almighty and eternal Father,
and in these days of Easter
to celebrate with joyful hearts
the memory of your wonderful works.
For by the mystery of his passion
Jesus Christ, your risen Son,
has conquered the powers of death and hell
and restored in men and women the image of your glory.
He has placed them once more in paradise
and opened to them the gate of life eternal.

And so, in the joy of this Passover,
earth and heaven resound with gladness,
while angels and archangels and the powers of all creation
sing for ever the hymn of your glory.
Holy, holy, holy Lord,
God of power and might,
heaven and earth are full of your glory.
Hosanna in the highest.
Blessed is he who comes in the name of the Lord.
Hosanna in the highest.

The president recalls the Last Supper,
and this acclamation is used

Jesus Christ is Lord:
Lord, by your cross and resurrection
you have set us free.
You are the Saviour of the world.

The Prayer continues and leads into the doxology,
to which all respond boldly

Amen.

The Lord's Prayer

Let us pray with confidence as our Saviour has taught us

Our Father, who art in heaven,
hallowed be thy name;
thy kingdom come;
thy will be done;
on earth as it is in heaven.
Give us this day our daily bread.
And forgive us our trespasses,
as we forgive those who trespass against us.
And lead us not into temptation;
but deliver us from evil.
For thine is the kingdom,
the power and the glory,
for ever and ever.
Amen.

Breaking of the Bread

The president breaks the consecrated bread.

We break this bread
to share in the body of Christ.
Though we are many, we are one body,
because we all share in one bread.

The Agnus Dei is sung as the bread is broken

Lamb of God,
you take away the sin of the world,
have mercy on us.
Lamb of God,
you take away the sin of the world,
have mercy on us.
Lamb of God,
you take away the sin of the world,
grant us peace.

Giving of Communion

The president gives the invitation to communion

Alleluia. Christ our passover is sacrificed for us.
Therefore let us keep the feast. Alleluia.

The president and people receive communion.

During the distribution a hymn and anthem are sung.

Prayer after Communion

The president says

Author of life divine,
in the resurrection of your Son,
you set before us the mystery of his triumph over sin and death;
may all who are washed in the waters of rebirth
rise to newness of life
and find the promised presence of your abundant grace;
through Jesus Christ our Lord.
Amen.   P3

*Following the Prayer after Communion the president gives some notices
relating to the life of the parish, including a reiteration of the
invitation for all to stay for a celebratory reception after the service.*

*The parents are invited to bring Joel out to the front of the church, and
they stand near the Paschal candle ready for the Sending Out.*

The Sending Out

The Blessing

The president gives the blessing

The Lord be with you
and also with you.

God the Father,
by whose glory Christ was raised from the dead,
strengthen you by his life-giving Spirit
to walk with him in the paths of righteousness and peace;
and the blessing of God almighty,
the Father, the Son, and the Holy Spirit,
be among you and remain with you always.
Amen.   *Q4*

Giving of a Lighted Candle

*A lighted candle is given to one of Joel's godparents to hold for him, with
the flame taken from the Paschal candle.*

The president then says

God has delivered us from the dominion of darkness
and has given us a place with the saints in light.

Joel, you have received the light of Christ;
walk in this light all the days of your life.
**Shine as a light in the world
to the glory of God the Father.**   *R1*

The Dismissal

The deacon leads the Dismissal

Go in the light and peace of Christ. Alleluia, alleluia!
Thanks be to God. Alleluia, alleluia!   *S1*

Hymn

*A final hymn is sung as Joel and his family return to their places,
and the ministers depart.*

Scenario 7 – St Anne's

Setting the scene

St Anne's is an evangelical church in the suburbs of a large city. As well as two morning services, there is also a well-attended evening service, which attracts large numbers of teenagers and young adults, including a significant number of students from the two universities in the city.

Twice a year St Anne's holds baptism services in this evening service. There are usually several candidates, almost always adults rather than infants. Sometimes the candidates include a number of people who are not being baptized but are renewing their baptism using the *Common Worship* material for Affirmation of Baptismal Faith. (See the guidance note above on using the Affirmation of Baptismal Faith material, pages 273–276.)

Notes on the service

Candidates

At this service, three young people are being baptized, Martha, Raj and Eloise.

Structure

The service structure is based on A Service of the Word to give maximum flexibility.

Mood and style

The mood and style of the service is informal (for instance, none of those involved in the service wear robes), and sung worship plays a large part. Songs and prayers are provided on a large screen at the front and on smaller screens placed in the main body of the church (on pillars). A video camera is used at key points in the baptism service, so the screens can also be used to make sure that everyone can see what is happening.

Mode of baptism

Baptisms at these evening services take place using a large portable baptism pool, which is placed prominently at the front of the church in the chancel. This area is where the choir stalls used to be, but is now where the worship band are set up, so the baptism pool is placed in front of them.

The general mode of baptism is by submersion, normally with the priest and the youth pastor on each side of the candidate, lowering them backwards into the water. However, for pastoral reasons, that mode is inappropriate for Eloise, and so she will be baptized by kneeling in the pool and having buckets of water poured over her instead.

The minister of baptism

When adults are being baptized, the bishop is always informed in advance, as required by Canon B 24. Sometimes, if possible, the bishop comes to preside at the service, and it can then include confirmation. In this case, the candidates will be confirmed at a deanery confirmation service next month, and because the baptism service itself is non-eucharistic, they will treat their confirmation as their admission to Holy Communion.

This service is, therefore, led by the curate, who is assisted for the baptisms themselves by the youth pastor, Mark (for Raj's baptism) and one of the youth leaders, Dulcie (for Martha and Eloise).

Sponsors

Each of the candidates has a sponsor or sponsors. These present the candidates to the congregation, join in signing them with the cross, and stand by the baptism pool ready to wrap their candidate in a towel when they come out of the pool.

Response to baptism

Adult baptisms can be emotional occasions, and there is an instinctive desire to respond immediately with enthusiasm, but in order to save the applause to the later Welcome of all the candidates together, at St Anne's they have added in an extra response ('Praise God for N's baptism / Alleluia!') which comes immediately after the baptism itself. This allows for a loud 'Alleluia' to express the natural joy felt by all.

Song

As well as a mix of contemporary worship songs, they use an older song (from 1980), 'River, wash over me' by Dougie Brown, as a sort of 'theme song' for the service. The song has three simple verses (River; Jesus; Spirit) and these are used at three points in the service: halfway through the Decision ('River, wash over me…'); at the end of the Decision, before the Signing with the Cross ('Jesus, rule over me…'); and after the Prayer for the Holy Spirit that follows the baptism ('Spirit, watch over me…'). Because the tune is simple, and it is repeated through the service, it makes it easier for visitors, who may not know the other songs, to join in.

Candles

St Anne's does not have an Easter candle, and they don't give out individual candles to baptism candidates (whether adults or infants), and so the Giving of a Lighted Candle section of the service is omitted.

The Service

Welcome and notices

The vicar welcomes everyone to the service and gives any important notices before handing over to the curate, who leads the rest of the service.

Opening praise

The curate gives an informal introduction explaining the meaning of baptism and explaining some of the practicalities, and then leads the opening ascription of praise

We stand before the throne of God
with countless crowds
from every nation and race, tribe and language.
Blessing and glory and wisdom,
thanksgiving and honour, power and might
be to our God for ever and ever.
Amen.

based on Revelation 7.9, 12

from New Patterns for Worship, *Section A, Call to Worship A24*

This leads into the first set of worship songs.

Worship songs

The Collect

The worship songs conclude with the curate leading an extempore prayer, based on this Collect

Heavenly Father,
by the power of your Holy Spirit
you give your faithful people new life in the water of baptism.
Guide and strengthen us by the same Spirit,
that we who are born again may serve you in faith and love,
and grow into the full stature of your Son, Jesus Christ,
who is alive and reigns with you
in the unity of the Holy Spirit
now and for ever.
Amen.   D1

Bible Reading

Sermon

Presentation of the Candidates

Martha, Raj and Eloise are invited to the front to be presented to the congregation by their sponsors.

Each sponsor (or group of sponsors) says, in turn
I present *Martha / Raj / Eloise* to be baptized.

The curate asks each of the candidates in turn
Martha / Raj / Eloise, do you wish to be baptized?

Each responds to the question with this
I do.   **F**1

Testimony by the candidates

The sponsors return to their seats.
Each candidate gives a brief testimony.

Congregational pledge

The curate addresses the whole congregation

Faith is the gift of God to his people.
In baptism the Lord is adding to our number
        those whom he is calling.
People of God at St Anne's,
will you welcome Martha, Raj and Eloise
and uphold them in their new life in Christ?
With the help of God, we will.   **F**2

The Decision

The curate addresses the candidates

In baptism, God calls us out of darkness into his marvellous light.
To follow Christ means dying to sin and rising to new life with him.

Therefore I ask:

Do you reject the devil and all rebellion against God?
I reject them.

Do you renounce the deceit and corruption of evil?
I renounce them.

Do you repent of the sins that separate us from God and neighbour?
I repent of them.

At this point, the curate and the candidates move closer to the baptism pool, and everyone sings the first verse of the song 'River wash over me, cleanse me and make me new' by Dougie Brown.

Do you turn to Christ as Saviour?
I turn to Christ.

Do you submit to Christ as Lord?
I submit to Christ.

Do you come to Christ, the way, the truth and the life?
I come to Christ.   *G1*

Another verse of the song is now sung: 'Jesus, rule over me, reign over all my heart…'

The Signing with the Cross

The curate makes the sign of the cross on the forehead of each candidate, saying

Christ claims you for his own.
Receive the sign of his cross.   *H1*

The sponsors are invited to the front, and each of them makes the sign of the cross on the forehead of the candidate they are sponsoring.

While this happens, musicians play the tune of 'River, wash over me' quietly in the background.

When all the candidates have been signed, the curate says

Do not be ashamed to confess the faith of Christ crucified.
Fight valiantly as a disciple of Christ
against sin, the world and the devil,
and remain faithful to Christ to the end of your life.   *H2*

May almighty God deliver you from the powers of darkness,
restore in you the image of his glory,
and lead you in the light and obedience of Christ.
Amen.   H3

Prayer over the Water

The curate stands close to the baptism pool, with the candidates
and their sponsors.

Loving Father,
we thank you for your servant Moses,
who led your people through the waters of the Red Sea
to freedom in the Promised Land.
We thank you for your Son Jesus,
who has passed through the deep waters of death
and opened for all the way of salvation.
Now send your Spirit,
that those who are washed in this water
may die with Christ and rise with him,
to find true freedom as your children,
alive in Christ for ever.
Amen.   I3

Profession of Faith

The curate introduces the Profession of Faith

Martha, Raj and Eloise are not being baptized into a general belief in
God, but into the specific Christian understanding of God, as
revealed to us in Jesus.

So, let us affirm,
together with Martha, Raj and Eloise, who are being baptized,
our common faith in Jesus Christ.

Do you believe and trust in God the Father,
source of all being and life,
the one for whom we exist?
I believe and trust in him.

Do you believe and trust in God the Son,
who took our human nature,
died for us and rose again?
I believe and trust in him.

Do you believe and trust in God the Holy Spirit,
who gives life to the people of God
and makes Christ known in the world?
I believe and trust in him.

This is the faith of the Church.
This is our faith.
We believe and trust in one God,
Father, Son and Holy Spirit.   J2

Baptism

The curate asks each candidate

Martha / Raj / Eloise, is this your faith?

Each of them answers in their own words, or

This is my faith.   K1

*The curate gets into the baptism pool, and is joined by Mark (for Raj's
baptism) and by Dulcie (for Eloise and Martha's). They help each
candidate into the pool and baptize them, either by lowering them into
the water, or pouring water on them. As they do so, the curate says*

Raj / Martha / Eloise, I baptize you in the name of the Father,
and of the Son,
and of the Holy Spirit.
Amen.   K2

After each candidate has been baptized, the curate leads this response

Praise God for *Raj's / Martha's / Eloise's* baptism!
Alleluia!

The curate then lays a hand on the candidate's shoulder and prays

Raj / Martha / Eloise,
may God, who has received you by baptism into his Church,
pour upon you the riches of his grace,
that within the company of Christ's pilgrim people
you may daily be renewed by his anointing Spirit,
and come to the inheritance of the saints in glory.
Amen.   K4

As each candidate climbs out of the baptism pool,
their sponsor wraps them in a towel, and they wait to witness the other
baptisms.

While one candidate gets out of the pool and the next gets in,
the congregation sing a final verse of the song 'River, wash over me':
'Spirit, watch over me, lead me to Jesus' feet…'.

When all three have been baptized, they are led by their sponsors to
places where they can change into dry clothes.

Worship songs

These include 'The Lord's my Shepherd, I'll not want' by Stuart Townend.

The curate invites everyone else, during these songs, to come forward
to the baptism pool if they would like to, and to dip their hand in the
water and apply it to their head or to make the sign of the cross with
the water on their forehead, as a reminder of their own baptism.

During the songs, the curate and others involved in the baptism also
change into dry clothes.

When Martha, Raj and Eloise have returned, they come to the front with
their sponsors.

The Welcome

There is one Lord, one faith, one baptism:
Martha, Raj and Eloise,
by one Spirit we are all baptized into one body.
**We welcome you into the fellowship of faith;
we are children of the same heavenly Father;
we welcome you.**   N1

The congregation greet the newly baptized with applause.

Each of the newly baptized is given a Bible as a gift from the church.

The Peace

The curate introduces the Peace in these or other suitable words.

We are all one in Christ Jesus.
We belong to him through faith,
heirs of the promise of the Spirit of peace.   N2

The peace of the Lord be always with you
and also with you.

Let's offer one another a sign of peace.

All may exchange a sign of peace.   **N**3

Prayers of Intercession

Martha, Raj and Eloise come to the front again, and stand with their
sponsors. Each sponsor is invited to offer an extempore prayer for their
candidate, or to read a prepared prayer.

The youth pastor prays for more general concerns, the needs of the
world, those who are sick, etc.

Martha, Raj and Eloise and their sponsors return to their seats.

The Lord's Prayer

The prayers conclude with the Lord's Prayer, led by the curate.

Song

Commission

The curate leads the newly baptized to the back of the church,
where they stand by the door.

The curate leads this Commission, which is addressed to Martha,
Raj and Eloise.

Those who are baptized are called to worship and serve God.

Will you continue in the apostles' teaching and fellowship,
in the breaking of bread, and in the prayers?
With the help of God, I will.

Will you persevere in resisting evil,
and, whenever you fall into sin, repent and return to the Lord?
With the help of God, I will.

Will you proclaim by word and example
the good news of God in Christ?
With the help of God, I will.

Will you seek and serve Christ in all people,
loving your neighbour as yourself?
With the help of God, I will.

Will you acknowledge Christ's authority over human society,
by prayer for the world and its leaders,
by defending the weak, and by seeking peace and justice?
With the help of God, I will.

May Christ dwell in your hearts through faith,
that you may be rooted and grounded in love
and bring forth the fruit of the Spirit.
Amen.   **L**3

The Blessing and Dismissal

The curate turns to address the whole congregation

The God of all grace,
who called you to his eternal glory in Christ Jesus,
establish, strengthen and settle you in the faith;
and the blessing of God almighty,
the Father, the Son, and the Holy Spirit,
be among you and remain with you always.
Amen.   **Q**1

Martha, Raj and Eloise say together

Let us go in peace, to love and serve the Lord.
In the name of Christ. Amen.

*Martha, Raj and Eloise stand by the door and greet the congregation as
they move through to the hall for refreshments.*

Scenario 8 – St Peter's

Setting the scene

Preparations are underway at St Peter's for the baptism of Jessica, a nine-month old baby. Jessica's birth was not easy, and her early weeks and months of life were filled with medical interventions and lots of anxiety for her parents. When they rang up to ask about a christening, it was clear that there was a deep-seated desire to thank God for bringing her through those early stages of her life.

St Peter's has a long-established pattern of offering a service of Thanksgiving for the Gift of a Child to all those who enquire about christening – either as first stage on the way to a planned baptism or sometimes as an alternative, particularly where parents are divided about whether they want their child baptized or not. Baptisms at St Peter's normally take place in a main Sunday service, and Thanksgivings are offered either as a stand-alone service on a Sunday afternoon or in a main Sunday service. Occasionally Thanksgivings have taken place in someone's home or in the function room of the nearby pub.

Jessica's parents had already asked a number of people to be godparents, including some who had provided special support to them in the early weeks of Jessica's life – either a shoulder to cry on, or more practical support. At the meeting with the vicar it became apparent that some of those people could not be godparents in a baptism because they were not baptized themselves – including their next-door neighbours, who are practising Sikhs. Because Jessica's parents were so keen to emphasize their gratitude to God, the vicar suggested that they combine a Thanksgiving for a Gift of a Child and a Baptism, having the service in a main Sunday act of worship. Jessica's parents could pick any number of people as supporting friends for the Thanksgiving part, and then a smaller selection as godparents for the baptism itself.

Notes on the service

Service structure

The service is a non-eucharistic morning service, using the framework of A Service of the Word, into which the key elements of the Thanksgiving for the Gift of a Child and the baptism service are integrated.

Supporting friends

There is the option in any baptism service to include a short Thanksgiving Prayer near the start. The option to include more elements from the Thanksgiving for the Gift of a Child is useful where parents want to make this a significant part of the service, and especially when they wish to acknowledge the role of a number of family and friends, not all of whom can be godparents. There are no restrictions on who can be a supporting friend in a Thanksgiving service, or on how many you can have. Their chief commitment is to the child and the family. They pledge their support 'with the help of God', but they do not have to make specific promises to support the child's Christian upbringing, or to lead by example in their own Christian practice.

In this case the larger group of supporting friends includes the smaller number who will also be godparents in the baptism part of the service, but it would be possible to have them as two distinct groups of people.

At St Peter's they keep a register of Thanksgiving Services, which includes a note of who the supporting friends were. The child is given a certificate, and each supporting friend is given a card with the child's name on it and the details of the service, with a reminder of the commitment they made to the family.

Though the terminology of 'supporting friends' is still new to most of those outside the Church, the clergy at St Peter's are keen to use it as it is the term used in the *Common Worship* service, and they wanted to avoid using 'sponsors' because of the potential for confusion with those who act as sponsors for baptism or confirmation.

The Service

Getting Ready

Greeting

Welcome in the name of Christ.
God's grace, mercy and peace be with you
and also with you.

from New Patterns for Worship, *Section A, Greeting A2*

The vicar gives informal welcomes and introductions.

Hymn or song

Collect Prayer

The vicar introduces a short time of silent prayer, and then prays the Collect of the Day.

Thanking God for the Gift of a Child

Introduction to
Thanksgiving for the Gift of a Child

The vicar invites Jessica, her parents and supporting friends to come to the front of the church, and then says

We rejoice today with Jessica's family
as they thank God for the gift of life
and bring her for baptism.

In this part of the service
we are going to give thanks to God for Jessica,
and to support her parents in their responsibilities
with prayer and love.   **B**3

Presentation for Thanksgiving

One of Jessica's parents explains something of the story of her birth, and introduces the supporting friends.

The vicar says to Jessica's parents and the supporting friends

Do you receive Jessica as a gift from God?
We do.
Do you wish to give thanks to God and seek his blessing?
We do.   **B**4

Thanksgiving Prayer

The vicar says this prayer

God our creator,
we thank you for the wonder of new life
and for the mystery of human love.
We thank you for all whose support and skill
surround and sustain the beginning of life.
We thank you that we are known to you by name
and loved by you from all eternity.
We thank you for Jesus Christ,
who has opened to us the way of love.
We praise you, Father, Son, and Holy Spirit.
Blessed be God for ever.   **B**5

Blessing of the Child

The vicar holds Jessica and says

As Jesus took children in his arms and blessed them,
so now we ask God's blessing on Jessica.

Heavenly Father, we praise you for Jessica's birth;
surround her with your blessing
that she may know your love,
be protected from evil,
and know your goodness all her days.
Amen.   **B**7

Pledge of support

*The vicar returns Jessica to her parents and says to the
supporting friends*

Will you do all that you can to help and support Joe and Natasha in
the bringing up of Jessica?
With the help of God, we will.

*The vicar turns to the wider family and friends, and the congregation,
and says*

Will you do all that you can to help and support this family?
With the help of God, we will.   **B**10

Jessica, her family and supporting friends, return to their places.

Children go to their learning activities as the next song is sung.

Song

Listening

Bible Reading

Sermon

Song or hymn

Baptizing

Introduction to Baptism

The vicar, using ideas from introduction C2, explains that in the next part of the service, Jessica will be baptized in water as a sign that she belongs not only to her family and friends, but to the family of the Church.

Jessica is brought to the front again, this time by her parents and godparents.

The vicar addresses the whole congregation

Jesus said, 'Let the children come to me. Do not stop them'.
We thank God for Jessica who has come to be baptized today.
Christ loves her and welcomes her into his Church.

So I ask you all:
Will you support Jessica as she begins her journey of faith?
We will.
Will you help her to live and grow within God's family?
We will.

The vicar turns to the parents and godparents and says

God knows each of us by name and we are his.
Parents and godparents, you speak for Jessica today.
Will you pray for her, and help her to follow Christ?
We will.   **F**4

The Decision

The Easter candle is lit.

The vicar addresses Jessica through her parents and godparents

We all wander far from God and lose our way:
Christ comes to find us and welcomes us home.
In baptism we respond to his call.

Therefore I ask:

Do you turn away from sin?
I do.
Do you reject evil?
I do.
Do you turn to Christ as Saviour?
I do.
Do you trust in him as Lord?
I do.   **G***2*

Signing with the Cross

The vicar makes the sign of the cross on Jessica's forehead, saying

Christ claims you for his own.
Receive the sign of his cross.   **H***1*

Do not be ashamed of Christ.
You are his for ever.
Stand bravely with him
against all the powers of evil,
and remain faithful to Christ to the end of your life.   **H***4*

May almighty God deliver you from the powers of darkness,
and lead you in the light and obedience of Christ.
Amen.   **H***5*

Song

A song is sung and everyone turns to face the font at the back of the church. The vicar leads Jessica and her parents and godparents to the font.

During the song, children return from their learning activities.

After the song, children are invited to come forward to the font so that they can see.

Prayer over the Water

We praise you, loving Father,
for the gift of your Son Jesus.
He was baptized in the River Jordan,
where your Spirit came upon him
and revealed him as the Son you love.
He sent his followers
to baptize all who turn to him.
Now, Father, we ask you to bless this water,
that those who are baptized in it
may be cleansed in the water of life,
and, filled with your Spirit,
may know that they are loved as your children,
safe in Christ for ever.
Amen.   14

Believing

The vicar introduces the Profession of Faith, inviting all those who share this belief to answer the questions along with the parents and godparents

Let us affirm,
together with Jessica, who is being baptized,
our common faith in Jesus Christ.

Do you believe and trust in God the Father,
source of all being and life,
the one for whom we exist?
I believe and trust in him.

Do you believe and trust in God the Son,
who took our human nature,
died for us and rose again?
I believe and trust in him.

Do you believe and trust in God the Holy Spirit,
who gives life to the people of God
and makes Christ known in the world?
I believe and trust in him.

This is the faith of the Church.
This is our faith.
We believe and trust in one God,
Father, Son and Holy Spirit.   *J2*

The Baptism

The vicar pours water on Jessica saying

Jessica Alana, I baptize you in the name of the Father,
and of the Son,
and of the Holy Spirit.
Amen.   *K2*

May God, who has received you by baptism into his Church,
pour upon you the riches of his grace,
that within the company of Christ's pilgrim people
you may daily be renewed by his anointing Spirit,
and come to the inheritance of the saints in glory.
Amen.   *K4*

The Welcome

There is one Lord, one faith, one baptism:
Jessica, by one Spirit we are all baptized into one body.
We welcome you into the fellowship of faith;
we are children of the same heavenly Father;
we welcome you.   *N1*

Everyone greets Jessica with applause.

Hymn

While the hymn is sung, everyone returns to their seats and turns to face the front of the church.

Commission

The vicar gives an informal commission, based on these key points

¶ *The welcome of the Church, local and universal*

¶ *The importance of belonging to the Christian community*

¶ *The responsibilities of parents and godparents*

¶ *The challenge to grow in Christian discipleship* **L2**

Prayers

The vicar leads this prayer for parents, godparents and supporting friends

Faithful and loving God,
bless those who care for Jessica,
including her parents, godparents and supporting friends,
and grant them your gifts of love, wisdom and faith.
Pour upon Jessica's family your healing and reconciling love,
and protect their home from all evil.
Fill them with the light of your presence
and establish them in the joy of your kingdom,
through Jesus Christ our Lord.
Amen.

adapted from **L5**

Further short prayers are led by a member of the congregation.

This response is used

Your name be hallowed.
Your kingdom come.

The Lord's Prayer

*The same member of the congregation leads everyone in saying the
Lord's Prayer*

As your children, born again in Christ, we say
Our Father ...   **M**1a

(For the full text of the Lord's Prayer, see back page.)

Going Out

*Jessica and her parents come to the front. They are given a candle, lit
from the Easter candle.*

The vicar says

God has delivered us from the dominion of darkness
and has given us a place with the saints in light.

You have received the light of Christ;
walk in this light all the days of your life.
**Shine as a light in the world
to the glory of God the Father.**   **R**1

Go in the light and peace of Christ.
Thanks be to God.

                                                                               S1

Authorization, Copyright and Acknowledgements

Authorization

Patterns for Baptism comprises:

- alternative services and other material authorized for use until further resolution of the General Synod;
- material commended by the House of Bishops.

For details, see page 387.

Canon B 3 provides that decisions as to which of the authorized services are to be used (other than occasional offices) shall be taken jointly by the incumbent and the parochial church council. In the case of occasional offices (other than Confirmation), the decision is to be made by the minister conducting the service, subject to the right of any of the persons concerned to object beforehand to the form of service proposed.

Copyright Information

The Archbishops' Council of the Church of England and the other copyright owners and administrators of texts included in *Patterns for Baptism* have given permission for the use of their material in local reproductions on a non-commercial basis which comply with the conditions for reproductions for local use set out in the Archbishops' Council's booklet, *A Brief Guide to Liturgical Copyright*. This is available from:

www.churchofengland.org/prayer-and-worship/copyright

A reproduction which meets the conditions stated in that booklet may be made without an application for copyright permission or payment of a fee, but the following copyright acknowledgement must be included:

> *Patterns for Baptism*, material from which is included in this service, is copyright © The Archbishops' Council 2022.

Permission must be obtained in advance for any reproduction which does not comply with the conditions set out in *A Brief Guide to Liturgical Copyright*. Applications for permission should be addressed to:

The Copyright Administrator
The Archbishops' Council
Church House
Great Smith Street
London SW1P 3AZ

E-mail: copyright@churchofengland.org

Acknowledgements and Sources

The publisher gratefully acknowledges permission to reproduce copyright material in this book. Every effort has been made to trace and contact copyright holders. If there are any inadvertent omissions we apologize to those concerned and undertake to include suitable acknowledgements in all future editions.

Published sources include the following:

The Archbishops' Council of the Church of England: *Common Worship: Christian Initiation* (Church House Publishing, 2006); *Common Worship: Christian Initiation: Additional Baptism Texts in Accessible Language* (Church House Publishing, 2015), both of which are copyright © The Archbishops' Council of the Church of England.

Cambridge University Press: Extracts (and adapted extracts) from *The Book of Common Prayer*, the rights in which are vested in the Crown, are reproduced by permission of the Crown's Patentee, Cambridge University Press.

The Division of Christian Education of the National Council of Churches in the USA: Unless otherwise stated, Scripture quotations are from The *New Revised Standard Version* of the Bible, copyright ©1989 by the Division of Christian Education of the National Council of Churches in the USA. Used by permission. All rights reserved.

The European Province of the Society of St Francis: 'As a royal priesthood let us pray to the Father' (pp. 115, 178, 191, 203, 218, 233, 245, 256) from *Celebrating Common Prayer*, copyright © The Society of St Francis European Province 1992 and 1996.

The Rt Revd David Stancliffe: The Proper Preface for Eucharist at a Baptism (pp. 129, 206, 220). Used by permission.

The General Synod of the Anglican Church of Canada: 'We thank you, almighty God, for the gift of water' (pp. 77, 187, 215, 229) and 'Will you continue in the apostles' teaching and fellowship' (pp. 107, 246, 257, 368), from *The Book of Alternative Services of the Anglican Church of Canada* © The General Synod of the Anglican Church of Canada 1985. Used by permission.

The English Language Liturgical Consultation: The Lord's Prayer, prepared by the English Language Liturgical Consultation, based on (or excerpted from) *Praying Together*, copyright © ELLC 1988.

Dave Gregory: *Messy Church Does Science* (BRF, 2017). Please see messychurch.org.uk for more details.

Common Worship:
The Baptism of Children in Accessible Language Card

The Additional Baptism Texts in Accessible Language aim to meet the spiritual needs of those who seek baptism for either themselves or their children, but who may not understand the church's traditional 'language' on the subject.

This service card presents the Holy Baptism service using these additional texts. It contains congregational responses rather than the full text of the service.

This card corresponds to Sample 1, as found on pages 171–180 of this volume

8 pages
ISBN 978 0 7151 2327 0

Common Worship:
Holy Baptism in Accessible Language with Holy Communion card

The Additional Baptism Texts in Accessible Language aim to meet the spiritual needs of those who seek baptism for either themselves or their children, but who may not understand the church's traditional 'language' on the subject.

This service card presents the text of the Holy Baptism in a Service of Holy Communion using these additional texts.

Please note a Holy Communion card or booklet is also required.

This card corresponds to Sample 3, as found on pages 181–192 of this volume.

6 pages
ISBN 978 0 7151 2332 4

Common Worship:
The Baptism of Children Card

Common Worship

The Baptism of Children

¶ *Preparation*

The grace of our Lord Jesus Christ,
the love of God
and the fellowship of the Holy Spirit
be with you all
All   **and also with you.**

Words of welcome or introduction may be said.

The president says the Collect.

¶ *The Liturgy of the Word*

Either one or two readings from Scripture may precede the Gospel.

At the end of each the reader may say

This is the word of the Lord.
All   **Thanks be to God.**

When the Gospel is announced the reader says

Hear the Gospel of our Lord Jesus Christ according to N.
All   **Glory to you, O Lord.**

At the end

This is the Gospel of the Lord.
All   **Praise to you, O Christ.**

The Sermon follows.

¶ *The Liturgy of Baptism*

Presentation of the Candidates

The candidates may be presented to the congregation.

The president addresses the whole congregation.

Faith is the gift of God to his people.
In baptism the Lord is adding to our number
    those whom he is calling.
People of God, will you welcome these children/candidates
    and uphold them in their new life in Christ?
All   **With the help of God, we will.**

The Baptism of Children   1

A service card including the text of the Holy Baptism service.
It contains congregational responses rather than the full text of the service.

Produced in a durable, tall, narrow format single-folded card with four panels.

This card corresponds to Sample 2, as found on pages 181–192 of this volume.

6 pages
ISBN 978 0 7151 2245 7

Common Worship: Baptism and Confirmation Services

This volume offers a complete collection of the authorised *Common Worship* baptism and confirmation services, including the Additional Baptism Texts in Accessible Language developed by the Liturgical Commission.

Suitable for use at the altar and font, it is designed to be used as a service book for baptism and confirmation and reflects the variety of practices in parishes and cathedrals.

It includes orders of service for:

- A stand alone service of baptism
- Baptism within Holy Communion
- Baptism at Easter Vigil
- Emergency Baptism
- Thanksgiving for the Gift of a Child
- Confirmation

480 pages
ISBN 978 0 7151 2352 2

The Lord's Prayer

As our Saviour taught us, so we pray

Our Father in heaven,
hallowed be your name,
your kingdom come,
your will be done,
on earth as in heaven.
Give us today our daily bread.
Forgive us our sins
as we forgive those who sin against us.
Lead us not into temptation
but deliver us from evil.
For the kingdom, the power,
and the glory are yours
now and for ever.
Amen.

(or)

Let us pray with confidence as our Saviour has taught us

Our Father, who art in heaven,
hallowed be thy name;
thy kingdom come;
thy will be done;
on earth as it is in heaven.
Give us this day our daily bread.
And forgive us our trespasses,
as we forgive those who trespass against us.
And lead us not into temptation;
but deliver us from evil.
For thine is the kingdom,
the power and the glory,
for ever and ever.
Amen.